# Nationalism

**Contributors**
Eugene Kamenka
John Plamenatz
George L. Mosse
F.X. Martin
Wang Gungwu
Shlomo Avineri

# Nationalism
## The nature and evolution of an idea

**Editor**
Eugene Kamenka

**ST. MARTIN'S PRESS    NEW YORK**

# Preface

In the past three years, the History of Ideas Unit in the Research School of Social Sciences of The Australian National University has presented an annual series of lectures on concepts or events in social and political spheres which combine past importance and contemporary intellectual relevance. The first series of lectures, presented in 1970 as the University Lectures for that year, was published under the title *A World in Revolution?* In that series, six historians and social theorists explored the nature and impact of revolutionary theory, revolutionary ideology and actual revolutions since the Great French Revolution of 1789. The second series, published under the title *Paradigm for Revolution?: The Paris Commune 1871-1971*, commemorated that short-lived but in many respects heroic revolt and considered its nature and historical significance. The lectures, and the books incorporating those lectures, have met with a gratifying response; *A World in Revolution?* is already in its third printing.

In July and August 1972 the History of Ideas Unit took advantage of the presence of three very distinguished Visiting Fellows from overseas working in the Unit – Professor Shlomo Avineri of the Hebrew University, Jerusalem, Professor George Mosse of the University of Wisconsin, and Professor John Plamenatz of All Souls College, Oxford – to arrange another very well attended series of public lectures on nationalism. These lectures are reprinted here, together with an extremely interesting paper on an aspect of Irish nationalism by another distinguished visiting academic, Professor Francis Xavier Martin of the National University of Ireland, who first read his paper to a History seminar in the Research School of Social Sciences. I am especially grateful to these visitors, who have agreed to allow us to publish their papers, to all the other participants in the series, to Miss W.G. Gordon and Mrs Rosemary Drury, who typed and arranged the manuscripts, and to Mrs E.Y. Short, research assistant in the History of Ideas Unit, who checked the manuscripts, compiled the index and read the proofs. For any errors that remain, I take responsibility.

*Canberra*                                              *Eugene Kamenka*

# Contents

# 1

# Political Nationalism–
# The Evolution
# of the Idea

*Eugene Kamenka*

The history of Europe since the French Revolution has been the history of the rise and development of political nationalism. In this century, history has become world history. Nationalism not only holds together the histories of the nineteenth and twentieth centuries, showing them to be part of a continuing crisis. It has also brought the histories of Asia, Africa and the Pacific into relation with European history, making them part of a universal history.

Nevertheless, nationalism is an extremely complex and difficult phenomenon, discomfiting to those who believe that lectures should begin with a definition of the subject. Nationalism can be, and has been, democratic or authoritarian, forward-looking or backward-looking, socialist or reactionary. As a conceptual tool, it often strikes the historian or political thinker as impossibly fuzzy: threatening to merge into patriotism or national consciousness at one end and fascism and anti-individualism at the other. Yet there would be something wrong with a history of modern Europe, or of the twentieth-century world, which made no use of the concept of nationalism.

Definitions, if they are useful at all, come at the end of an inquiry and not at the beginning. In the study of history and society they provide no substitute for grasping a phenomenon in all the complexity of its historical and social development. We need, initially, not the analytical skills of the philosopher but the historian's sense of connection, novelty and 'feel'. For nationalism, as a political ideology, as an 'ism', is above all a specific historical phenomenon, to be distinguished as such from the much more general sense of patriotism or national consciousness. It is best understood by examining the specific conditions under which it arose and developed and in which it came to differentiate itself from mere patriotism or national consciousness. To say this, is not to commit the genetic fallacy; it is simply to insist on the historical content and dimension of social and political concepts.

Nationalism, we shall be arguing, is a modern and initially a European phenomenon, best understood in relation to the developments that produced, and were symbolised by, the French Revolution of 1789. This is not to say that the rise of political nationalism as a modern phenomenon had no preconditions. Those who attempt to deal with history and politics in terms drawn from social and individual psychology, and those who are anxious to discredit nationalism by emphasising its atavistic character, assimilate it to what they see as a universal phenomenon in human history — tribalism. Certainly, men do confront us — even before the rise of dynastic empires and nation-states — as divided into populations or tribes, with their distinctive speech or dialect, peculiar patterns of social organisation and cultural and religious observance, special sets of oral traditions and manners of initiating their youthful members into the full life and lore of the tribe and of thus inculcating in them a supreme loyalty to it. Certainly, too, we can see that such tribal consciousness, such proto-nationalism if you like, survived to some extent into the empires, dynasties and city states that dominated much of the literary history of mankind as local patriotism and could become, among fringe peoples, a form of national consciousness. The Jews symbolised their tribal unity and their sense of national mission in the concept of Jehovah, the god of His people, and thus came very much closer to a modern nationalism than most peoples in antiquity. Certainly, they took pride in producing a typical nationalist manifesto — that mixture of folklore, ethical exhortation and nationalist political propaganda that we call the Bible. The Vietnamese and Koreans, under Chinese pressure, also developed an unusually strong national feeling early in their history. The Greeks, in a somewhat weaker form of national consciousness closer to tribalism, had a concept of Hellas and divided the known world — the *oikomene* — into Greeks and barbarians. The Chinese distinguished the Middle Kingdom, the Centre of the World (inhabited by Chinese) from the outer barbarism inhabited by others. This sort of tribal or national consciousness, this tendency to distinguish between in-group and out-group, can be found throughout human history. Medieval universities and the medieval church, which came to use the word *nation* with a technical significance as an organisational unit, were drawing on such feelings.

In the University of Prague, founded in 1348, the students were divided into German, Czech and Polish *nationes*; in the University of Aberdeen they were divided into the four nations of Mar, Buchan, Moray and Angus (regions of north-eastern Scotland); in Paris, the University recognised the 'nations' of France, Picardie, Normandie and Germany. In Dante's Italy, the expressions *nazione fiorentina* or *nazione milanese* were used. At times, this sense of in-group solidarity, of tribal or even national consciousness in the face of another tribe or out-group, could become very strong. There were such occasions, as we have seen, in the history of the Jews, of the Vietnamese, of the Koreans. There were similar occasions in the history of the ancient Egyptians, of the Greeks, the Armenians and the Persians. In Europe, by the late Middle Ages, acute consciousness of nationality could be evinced and was evinced by Italians and Greeks in the Fourth Crusade, by Frenchmen and Provençaux in the Albigensian Crusade, by Slavs and Teutons in their fifteenth-century conflicts, by Frenchmen and Englishmen in the concluding phases of the Hundred Years' War. For most of recorded history, nevertheless, from 500 B.C. to about A.D. 1700, the nation and the tribe did not command the supreme loyalty and patriotism of civilised man. The diffusion of agricultural and industrial techniques (the domestication of animals and plants, the expanding use of copper, iron and boats), the conquest and consolidation of tribes by military empires, the spread of inter-tribal religions such as Buddhism, Christianity or Islam and the development of literary languages, such as Sanskrit, Greek, Latin and Chinese, facilitated the creation of supra-tribal empires and loyalties.

In these circumstances, as Carlton J. Hayes put it forty years ago,[1]

... tribalism was largely supplanted by either cosmopolitanism or localism. The masses, fused together from various tribes and yet marked off from the upper classes by economic, social and cultural discrimination, were usually quite local in experience and loyalty; their supreme patriotism was directed toward the agricultural estate or village, the commercial town or the petty feudal province in which they lived and labored. On the other hand, the upper classes, while they might be intensely loyal to city-state, to duchy or to county, were apt to associate a higher patriotism with an area and with ideas which covered more than the primitive tribes and even the larger aggregates which in modern times are called nationalities; in their cosmopolitanism they were devoted to the fusion of peoples in a common empire, a common religion or a common culture. For at least sixty centuries of recorded history warfare was not generally between such nationalities as have waged war in the last two centuries but between cities and provinces of kindred nationality or between international empires or religions. The conquests of the Roman Empire, the internecine struggles among the Greek city-states, the

[1] Carlton J. Hayes, 'Nationalism. Historical Development', in Edwin R.A. Seligman (ed.), *Encyclopaedia of the Social Sciences,* New York, 1933, vol. 11, p. 240, on which I have also drawn in the preceding paragraph and in part of what follows.

private feudal combats of the Middle Ages, the protracted crusading conflict of Christendom with Islam, displayed less the character of modern nationalism than that of ancient or medieval cosmopolitanism or localism.

Not only nationalism, then, but even tribalism, localism and national consciousness are specific historical phenomena, not mere abstract expressions of the human spirit but movements and sentiments with specific social and historical content, deriving from specific social and historical conditions. To say this, of course, is not to say that tribalism, localism and national consciousness can be distinguished from each other without any demarcation disputes arising, or can be arranged in a neat historical schematism in which tribalism always precedes localism and in which localism always precedes national consciousness. Special conditions could and did produce something very like nations and nation-states at particular times before the modern period; but the concept of the nation and the nation-state as the *ideal, natural* or *normal* form of international political organisation, as the focus of men's loyalties and the indispensable framework for all social, cultural and economic activities became widespread only at a specific historical period. It emerged — slowly — in Europe, out of the ruins of the Roman Empire. Augustine, in his *De civitate dei* (IV, 15), had expressed the hope that the Roman Empire would be replaced by a world of small states. This, indeed, was what happened. For a period, however, Roman and Christian traditions proved stronger than the inroads of the barbarians and the psychological consequences of the sack of Rome. The definitive breach between ancient society and medieval society, as Henri Pirenne has argued, did not occur until the collapse of the Carolingian Empire and the then accelerated development of the preconditions for a world of nation-states. The Frankish historian Frechulf, Bishop of Lisieux, was perhaps the first to abandon the hitherto sacred conception that all political legitimacy rested in the continued existence of the Roman Empire and to assert that the founding of a new kingdom on Roman territory marked the beginning of a new era in history. It was not till the twelfth century, however, which saw a remarkable flowering of the beginnings of true national consciousness in a whole series of European countries, that this view became influential. In France, the Capetian kings were suddenly hailed in a novel way as national heroes fighting English and German invaders; the French victory at Bouvines in 1214 let loose a flood of national exultation that would have been unthinkable only 150 years earlier. In Italy and Sicily national feeling arose, again in the twelfth century, as a reaction to German aggression. The Chanson de Roland

and Geoffrey of Monmouth's *History of the Kings of Britain,* the most famous and influential 'nationalist historiography of the Middle Ages', fixed in writing the new burgeoning of national consciousness. Polish history and Polish nationhood were extolled, in the shape of Casimir I, by Magister Vincentius; the first two histories of Denmark were produced, under commission by Archbishop Absalon, by Saxo Grammaticus and Sven Aggeson. In Germany, Walter von der Vogelweide composed a poem in honour of the German people, extolling the superiority of their civilisation and of their women.[2]

From the fourteenth to the eighteenth centuries in Europe this rise of national consciousness and of a feeling that nations are the basic social and cultural units of society gained force. Economic developments were transforming the domestic economy of the rural manor and the urban guild into a national economy. Feudal and interurban warfare were gradually supplanted by warfare on a larger scale, warfare between nations, though still commonly for the dynastic aggrandisement of monarchs. Such monarchs were becoming symbols of national power and prestige, while the upper and middle classes were becoming more enthusiastic exponents of national, as against local or cosmopolitan interests. In other words, again those used by Carlton Hayes, nationalism emerges from

> an extraordinary complex of economic, political, social and intellectual developments: the invention and spread of printing; the rise of national vernaculars as literary languages, accompanied by the decline of Latin and other international languages; the revolutionary growth of capitalism and the middle classes, the role of aggressive divine right monarchs in suppressing feudalism and in consolidating and secularizing their realms on a national basis; the religious upheavals which eventuated in the disruption of Christendom and the establishment of state churches.

By the eighteenth century, such sentiments had reached their highest point of development in England, where geographical situation and historical circumstance combined to make the country most fully a nation, with a parliament and an aristocracy and an upper middle class that saw its own interest and the national interest as coinciding completely.

Nevertheless, when the French Revolution of 1789 asserted the principle of national self-determination as the basis for the new political order in Europe, it was doing something very frightening and very revolutionary. National consciousness had grown remarkably in Europe

[2] See Halvdan Kocht, 'The Dawn of Nationalism in Europe', in *The American Historical Review,* vol. 52 (1946/7), pp. 265-80, where these and other examples are cited.

between the twelfth century and the eighteenth, but generally speaking
the nation had not yet become the clear focus of loyalty for the inhabitants of a state; outside Britain especially, they were subjects rather than
citizens. Nationalism was a new word and a new concept, first used in
1798 in the famous *Mémoires pour servir à l'histoire du Jacobinisme*
written in exile in London by the fiercely anti-Jacobin French priest
Augustin Barruel. Barruel recognised the revolutionary nature of that
new ideology, *nationalisme* (then still commonly called *patriotisme*); he
saw that it meant to overthrow legitimate governments whose claim to
authority was based on divine ordination and/or hereditary rights; he
linked it with the, to him, terrible spirit of freemasonry and enlightenment, rooted in egoism. Barruel, purporting to reproduce a speech by
Adam Weishaupt, leader of what Barruel regarded as that sinister Maso-
nic sect, the Illuminati (who counted Goethe and Herder among their
members and who were, of course, suppressed by the Bavarian government in 1784), writes:

> At the moment in which men combined in nations . . . they ceased to
> recognise one another under a common name. *Nationalism,* or the
> love of nation (*l'amour national*), took the place of the love of
> mankind in general (*l'amour général*) . . . It became a virtue to
> extend [one's territories] at the expense of those who did not belong
> to one's empire. It became permissible, in order to achieve this, to
> despise strangers, to deceive them, to injure them. This virtue was
> called *Patriotism* . . . and if this is so, why not define this love yet
> more narrowly? . . . Thus, one saw *Patriotism* giving birth to *Localism*
> [Particularism] or the spirit of family, and finally to *Egoism*. [3]

Fifty years later, in 1849, the word nationalism was being heard often
enough. In that year, a much more distinguished exile than Barruel
reflected on 'isms'. Prince Metternich, his power ended, his system torn
asunder by the revolutions of 1848, was living in retirement in Brussels.
There he had a very interesting conversation indeed with the militant
Catholic Louis Veuillot, editor of *L'Univers*, subsequently a spirited
defender of those two modern Catholic tragedies — the doctrine of Papal
infallibility and the promulgation of the Syllabus of Errors. 'When the
French language adds *isme* to a substantive', Metternich told Veuillot,
'it adds to the thing mentioned an idea of scorn and degradation'. Metternich had no difficulty in thinking of examples: 'theism', 'liberalism' and
'*nationalism*'. In matters linguistic, however, as in matters political,
Metternich was not entirely without principles. The rule about *isms*, he

[3] For this citation, and the conversation with Metternich that follows, see G. de
Bertier de Sauvigny, 'Liberalism, Nationalism and Socialism: The Birth of Three
Words', in *The Review of Politics*, vol. 32 (1970), pp. 147-66 at pp. 155 and 150.

was prepared to admit, also applied to 'catholicism' and 'royalism'. Under the banner of catholicism one found people more catholic than the church; under the banner of royalism people more monarchical than the king. For Metternich, ideologising was dangerous in itself.

Nevertheless, in 1849 as in 1814, the great architect of the Continental system was looking backward not forward. Isms, including nationalism or at least the principle of nationality, were already winning the day. Men were becoming Italians, Germans, Frenchmen, etc. Fifty years after Metternich's conversation with Veuillot, one hundred years after Augustin Barruel's *Mémoires,* the Russian philosopher Vladimir Solovyev published a book entitled *The Justification of the Good. An Essay in Moral Philosophy* (St Petersburg, 1897). Solovyev was no less religious and no less a moraliser than Augustin Barruel, and very much less a fanatic, but by 1897 it seemed perfectly natural and proper to include a chapter entitled 'The National Question from the Moral Point of View'. In it, Solovyev wrote:

> Let it be granted that the immediate object of the moral relation is the individual person. But one of the essential peculiarities of that person – the direct continuation and expansion of his individual character – is his nationality (in the positive sense of character, type and creative power). This is not merely a physical, but also a psychological and moral fact. At the stage of development that humanity has now reached, the fact of belonging to a given nationality is to a certain extent confirmed by the individual's self-conscious will. Thus nationality is an inner, inseparable property of the person – something very dear and close to him. It is impossible to stand in a moral relation to this person without recognising the existence of what is so important to him. The moral principle does not allow us to transform a concrete person, a living man with his inseparable and essential national characteristics, into an empty abstract subject with all his determining peculiarities left out. If we are to recognise the inner dignity of the particular man, this obligation extends to all positive characteristics with which he connects his dignity; if we love a man we must love his nation, which he loves and from which he does not separate himself.

In 1920 there were many men and women of good will to whom this would have sounded strikingly old-fashioned; today it sounds modern again.

## II

The French Revolution was above all the revolt against the *ancien régime,* against the old order of men and societies. It rebelled against kings and estates in the name of the people. As part of that rebellion the concept of 'nation' acquired a largely new *political* significance.

Since kings were to cease governing and 'people' were to take their place, people had to be moulded into some sort of unity, defined and limited in some sort of way. The concept of 'nation' thus came to the fore as a *fundamental political category*.

In Rousseau's concept of the general will, as another of our contributors, Professor Mosse, has put it, the people came to worship themselves, declared themselves the source of all sovereignty. The king had obviously been a unity, a single person; the people, the new sovereign, would also have to be defined, given limits or personality as a 'nation'. Thus, in elevating the concept of citizen, the French Revolution came to elevate the concept of the nation. In its wars against the surrounding dynastic kingdoms and principalities, in its emphasis on popular sovereignty, it stood — at least officially — for the principle of national self-determintion. To the men who made the French Revolution, however, 'nation' remained a practical political category rather than a metaphysical one. A nation, for them, was a political-administrative unit, an aggregate of individuals able to participate in a common political life through their use of a common language and their physical propinquity to each other. As Abbé Siéyès put it in 1789, a nation 'is a union of individuals governed by one law, and represented by the same law-giving assembly'. The *basic* concept of the French Revolution was not that of the *Frenchman*, but that of the *citoyen*. When the new rulers of France had to decide whether Jews, too, were Frenchmen, they did not ask whether the Jews had taken part in a common heritage; they asked only whether the Jews could take part in the common work of the future, whether there was any respect in which they would place themselves outside the polity of all Frenchmen.

The Revolution and the Napoleonic campaigns that consummated the French sense of nationhood and gave France and Frenchmen renewed confidence made Germans aware of their disunity and their political backwardness. Germany lacked not only a French Revolution, but even a Louis XIV. The glory of the French was the *Notstand*, the state of emergency, of Germany. (The German *Not*, with its strong suggestion of imminent disaster, has become in English the weak word *need*; if we attend to the contrast in historical situations that has produced the difference in meaning between these two words, we will understand the past complacency of the English and the desperation of the Germans.) Thus, while France turned from the Cult of Reason to the Cult of Napoleon, a generation of Germans whose thought was as influential as that of Lessing, Goethe and Kant set about creating the cult of nationalism. For Fichte, Herder, Novalis and Schleiermacher, and later for

Savigny, nations were not mere conglomerations of individuals or convenient administrative units. Nations were organisms of which the individual was a subordinate part; outside such an organism he had no life. The divisions between nations were thus fundamental human divisions, analogous to the division of species in the animal kingdom. These divisions were laid down and determined by God and Nature; man could not escape them. Dynastic rulers had divided Germany instead of uniting her; nations, therefore, could not simply be based on states, on actual political arrangements. Nations were determined by language and history. 'Every language', Schleiermacher wrote, 'is a particular mode of thought, and what is cogitated in one language can never be repeated in the same way in another'. The first task confronting Germany was not democracy, not popular sovereignty, but unity, a revival of the 'German spirit'. To the French concept of the *citoyen* the Germans counterposed a concept that was to become the core of Nazism, but also of most modern nationalist movements, the concept of *Volksgenosse,* of the man who shares your blood, your language, your history and your national aspirations. As Rudolf Hess is reported to have said at the Parteitag der Ehre in September 1936, where he 'honoured' forty-eight flags of the Nazi Auslandsorganisation,

> The Führer has come in order to hammer into all of us the fact that the German cannot and may not choose whether or not he will be German, but that he was sent into this world by God as a German, and that God thereby has laid upon him, as a German, duties of which he cannot divest himself without committing treason to Providence. Therefore, we believe and we know that the German everywhere is a German — whether he lives in the *Reich*, or in Japan, in France or in China, or anywhere else in the world. Not countries or continents, not climate or environment, but blood and race determine the world of ideas of the German.

German nationalism is in important respects a rather special phenomenon. Since the break-up of the first Holy Roman Empire, the German-speaking peoples had failed to find and maintain a political unity such as Prussia began trying to impose in the nineteenth century. The Reformation that had made other peoples into nations had fatally split Germany into two cultural and political camps. At the same time, German power declined as the Swedes, the Dutch and the French successfully blocked her from major participation in world trade. In consequence, as Hans Kohn has stressed, Germany was in a very real sense shut out from Europe, left brooding in a semi-medieval darkness, lit up only by petty princes and their retinues. German nationalism thus became not only a demand for the creation of a German political nation, but also for the primacy of that nation among the European powers. While other people were becoming nation-states, Germany had gone through its 'schreckliche kaiserlose Zeit' in the fourteenth century; it came to look back on the Hohenstauffen emperors with their domains in Italy and Sicily as the true symbols of German imperial greatness. Hence German nationalism has never aimed at a rationally circumscribed polity, but at a *Reich.* Germany's malady was that she had not become part of modern western Europe; for much of the last hundred years, she proposed to cure this malady by absorbing Europe instead of being absorbed by it.

### III

Nations arise by historical accident, that is as the result of various factors not linked to each other by iron necessity. It is not true that men, early in their history, were divided into nations and that each such Ur-nation contained within itself, from the very beginning, a subsequent national destiny. Peoples and races have formed under specific geographical and social conditions; they have been scattered, mixed and re-formed. Nations have arisen most commonly around a centralised state; the boundaries of that state have been the result of various and often unrelated factors. Language, territory, religion, economic ties, political authority and racial origin have all done their work and left their mark; but none of these can be treated as decisive. It is not true that 'blood' determines ideas, or that 'race' is unaffected by environment. In his famous lecture *Qu'est-ce qu'une nation?* of 1882, Ernest Renan recognised that nations cannot be defined simply as ethnographical or linguistic groups. According to Renan, a nation is based on two things. First, it must have a sense of common history, particularly a memory of common sufferings which seem more important than the conflicts and divisions also to be found within that history. Secondly, the people concerned must have a will to live together: 'To have done great things together, and the will to do more, these are the essential conditions for a people . . . The existence of a nation is . . . a daily plebiscite.'

The conditions under which nationhood arises cannot be laid down in advance. The point of Renan's definition is to insist on the conscious, psychological nature of the *sense* of nationhood. The sense may arise in many different ways and there are no clear things that people must have in common in order to become, even emotionally, a nation. In France, a French nation and a sense of nationhood were gradually formed from the synthesis of Bretons, Normans, Provençaux, Burgundians, Flemings, Germans, Basques and Catalans. The synthesis itself was primarily created by political power, by the success of the Capetian kings in extending their originally small territorial base in the Ile de France, creating a 'French' monarchy, and in resisting what came to be seen as 'English' and 'German' aggression. Political power, aided by geography, created the 'English' nation out of Britons, Angles, Saxons, Jutes and Danes and succeeded in absorbing the Norman conquerors, as it is absorbing the Scottish nation and, with somewhat more trouble, the Welsh, today. All nations tend to believe that there are certain essential characteristics that bind them together and distinguish them from other nations, while the differences within the nation are treated as secondary and inessential. But what is essential and what is inessential, what could become the nucleus of a feeling of nationhood and what could not, is a matter of detailed historical conditions, a matter, that is, of historical accident.

In England, the very considerable tensions that existed for almost two centuries between protestants and papists did not threaten the existence of the nation as a nation, even though there were those who were willing to turn to external powers in order to save England from continuing heresy. On the other hand, in the state that is now Yugoslavia the primary tensions between inhabitants, and their claims to belong to different 'nations', rested on religion and became converted into so-called national differences as the ideology of nationalism spread. The Catholic Croats distinguished themselves from the Orthodox Serbs who spoke the same Serbo-Croat language, while the Moslems of Bosnia, who also speak Serbo-Croat, insisted, on coming under Austrian rule in 1878, that they were a separate Moslem nation. In modern Algeria, Berber and Arab, two separate and long antagonistic 'nations', in their struggle against the French suddenly saw themselves as and became one nation: the Moslems of Algeria as against the French of Algeria. Most frequently, it is true, nations have arisen on a linguistic basis; but in some cases, at least, the language has been created for them by nationalist intellectuals. There was no Slovak nation before the nineteenth century, when a standardised Slovak literary language was created from the various Slav dialects spoken by peasants in the mountain valleys of Northern Hungary. Ukrainian nationalism has depended heavily on the virtual creation of a Ukrainian literary language by the nineteenth-century poet Taras Shevchenko. Czechoslovakia, it has been said — only half jokingly — was invented by an eminent English historian. In Turkey, the modern nationalist revolutionaries made a real and contingent choice between a Pan-Turkic nationalist movement based on the Osmanli and the Turkish nationalism of the Anatolian peasant, the *Türk*. In the

Soviet Union, on the other hand, the Turkic peoples have been divided into separate 'nations' by a deliberate Soviet policy which halted the late nineteenth-century movement toward creating a common Turkic literary language and instead artificially magnified Turkic dialects into Uzbek, Turkmen, Kirgiz, Kazakh, and Kara-Kalpak languages.

What I have been arguing towards, then, is this. With the break-up of dynastic empires there comes a radical change in the basis of political sovereignty and in the kind of legitimacy sought and claimed by political institutions. The concept of popular sovereignty replaces the concept of the divinely or historically appointed ruler; the concept of the citizen replaces the concept of the subject. But in establishing the institutions of popular sovereignty, it is necessary to define what is the populace: self-government requires a community that is to be the self. In some, more fortunate, countries this community was established and defined for all practical purposes before the transition to representative government. Cromwell, the French revolutionaries and the men who sought the federation and independence of Australia could take the existence of a national community for granted. In the Ottoman Empire, in Austro-Hungary (which contained, as Musil said, many departments, institutions, languages and races, but only one nation — the Hungarian), in the lands dominated by Russia and in many of the European possessions overseas it was otherwise. Here the actual communities established by various social, linguistic and sentimental ties did not correspond to the formal political unities or divisions; here the demand for popular sovereignty was accompanied by a fundamental problem of defining the nation or community that was to exercise this sovereignty.

In these circumstances, then, we find the rise of a true *political* nationalism turning its attention inward to the organisation and basis of the polity as opposed to mere national consciousness or even nationalistic xenophobia, which arises from external threats and fears. In the fortunate countries in which the community has a political unity clearly defined before the transition to popular government, there may be strong feelings of national pride, suspicion of foreigners, even a strong element of jingoism in response to what is seen as an external danger. But nationalism as a political movement normally does not arise on a scale sufficient to make it a central issue in political life. One does not agitate for that which one already has. It is where men feel strongly a discrepancy between their sense of community and the actual political arrangements of which they are part, that political nationalism develops as an integral and fundamental part of the demand for popular sovereignty. Here nationalism attempts to create a correspondence between sense of community and economic and political organisation by irredentism (the 'liberation' of Sicily, the *Anschluss* of Austria) and/or by expelling or assimilating through the strongest ideological pressure what are seen as alien elements with conflicting interests (Egypt, Uganda, etc.). For while minorities organised as communities can be subjects, modern history has shown that it is very difficult for them to be citizens.

Historically, then, modern political nationalism arises in the course of stabilising or making possible the transition from autocratic to democratic or at least popular government. It is a re-casting and re-formation of communities and of political boundaries in circumstances where the old basis of the polity has been radically undermined.

## IV

'Nationalism', one of its most distinguished students, Hans Kohn, has written, 'is a political creed that underlies the cohesion of modern societies and legitimizes their claim to authority. Nationalism centers the supreme loyalty of the overwhelming majority of the people upon the nation-state, either existing or desired.' [4] In the opening section of this paper, I attempted to sketch briefly the continuous growth of national feeling or national consciousness — nationalism in a weak sense — which began in Europe in the twelfth century. That growth was inextricably intertwined with major social and economic developments which produced the nation-state. The French Revolution politicised national consciousness by making it the logical foundation for the changeover from subject to citizen. Where the conditions for a nation-state were already clearly present, such consciousness remained a sentiment rather than an ideology — it remained nationalism in the weak sense. Where they were not, tribal, local or national feelings acquired an energising charge, developed into nationalism in the strong sense, into a political ideology that becomes the first and major item on the democratic agenda. This is what happened in Greece, Poland, Italy, Hungary, Ireland, etc., and in South America during the nineteenth century and in Asia, Africa and the Pacific during the twentieth.

Precisely because political nationalism in these latter conditions, was the first item on the democratic agenda, Karl Marx, the greatest of all nineteenth-century European internationalists, spent as much time attending meetings to support or commemorate Polish and Irish struggles for independence as he spent organising or supporting strikes. The creation of the nation-state as a precondition for, or part of, the creation of a democratic polity — the struggle for national independence and for

[4] Hans Kohn, 'Nationalism', in David L. Sills (ed.), *International Encyclopedia of the Social Sciences*, New York, 1968, vol. 11, p. 63.

the fragmentation of supranational autocracies – had his support and that of most socialists. Socialists and liberals admired Mazzini, but they hated Bismarck, much as socialists and liberals later admired Nasser and Kenyatta while hating Franco and Vorster. Nationalism, for them, had a dark side and a light side, a reactionary one and a progressive one. Thus the Jewish liberal nationalist Simon Dubnow insisted, early in this century, that the sentiments that were progressive nationalism in the Jew were reactionary chauvinism in the Great Russian. The distinction had to be made in terms of the objective historical situation of the nation concerned. For nations whose national territory was secure and whose state had long been created, nationalism was a reactionary reversion to primitive hates; for nations that politically were not yet nations, that were oppressed or fragmented, for men whose nationhood still lay in the future, nationalism was a necessary step on the path to progress. In the eyes of such socialists and liberals, then, nationalism was never an end in itself: it was a means towards human development. Some nations had been fortunate and had gained their territorial and political status before the demand grew for popular sovereignty; they could settle down, needing little more than a modest glow of pride in their history and culture, to the task of economic and political progress and to friendly co-operation with other nations. Nationalism was for the deprived, for the unfortunate, for those who still had to find or create the conditions for their own dignity. As Dubnow put it in his discussion of Solovyev:

> Solovyev, the representative of the Russian people, is right in rejecting the 'fanatical concern for one's own nation'. He is right from the point of view of *his* nationality, since the ruling Russian nationality does not need such concern; it is useful only to the fanatics who have adopted the slogan of 'Russia for the Russians'. But Solovyev would be entirely wrong were he to extend his condemnation also to the national minorities in Russia, who can only maintain themselves if they are 'concerned for their own national individuality'. In the case of a nationality which is persecuted or which lacks political liberty it is perfectly reasonable to encourage a group of nationalists, because such a nationality must fight for its national character and its autonomy against the ruling nationality which seeks to weaken it or swallow it up. When the ruling nationality in the state, however, sets up groups of 'nationalists' of its own, it is bent not on defence but on attack, and it seeks to strengthen its rule by crushing the freedom of the subject nationalities; it wants to turn its national minorities into Germans, Russians, Poles, etc., and to force them to adopt its language, its educational system, its political aspirations . . . We are all in the habit of associating this kind of nationalism and patriotism with violence and oppression and with political despotism, and we understand perfectly well why our liberal friends among the ruling

nationalities emphatically declare: 'We are not nationalists and we are not "patriots"!' The word 'patriots' is put in quotation marks to indicate that there is also a reputable kind of patriotism . . . It would be advisable to use quotation marks also for the extreme nationalism of aggressive groups.[5]

Modern history, I believe, stands in the shadow of two momentous events whose implications are still working themselves out in time: the Industrial Revolution and the French Revolution. These two revolutions cannot be treated singly or separately, as though one provided the material, economic base of modern society and the other the intellectual, political base. The Industrial Revolution and the French Revolution were, in Europe, part and parcel of the one development: each was to work out its further implications in relation to the other, each embodied a universal drive that made them spread far beyond Europe and European societies. The 'logic' of commercialism, scientific culture and the industrial process, working itself out in a specific, initially European context, led to vastly accelerated economic, scientific and industrial change and development, followed in the twentieth century by the ever-increasing economic role of the state, by the widespread acceptance and institutionalisation of economic calculation and social and economic planning. The conception and the reality of economic progress were to change the face of the world. The same was true of the conception of political progress.

The French Revolution, as Alexis de Tocqueville wrote in a famous passage of his *L'Ancien régime et la révolution,* was the first 'universal' political revolution. It gave

the impression of striving for a renewal of mankind and not merely for the reform of France. It has therefore kindled a passion such as even the most violent political revolutions have not hitherto been able to produce. It started a proselytising campaign and brought propaganda into the world. In this way, it eventually assumed a religious character, which astonished contemporaries. Even more, it became itself a kind of religion . . . one which has flooded the world with its fighters, its apostles and its martyrs.

The French Revolution has proved to be what Hegel called a world-historical event: it symbolised, politically, the birth of the modern era. Like the Industrial Revolution it contained within itself the seeds of innumerable subsequent revolutions; politically it gave the world the very

[5] Simon Dubnow, 'The Ethics of Nationalism', being Letter III in *Letters on Old and New Judaism* (1897-1907), transl. in Simon Dubnow, *Nationalism and History,* ed. Koppel S. Pinson, New York, 1961, pp. 125-6.

idea of Revolution, of cataclysmic progress, an idea that proved more powerful and more important than that other eighteenth-century invention — the idea of Happiness. The world that followed the French upheaval of 1789, as Hegel saw, stood under the category of the *Incomplete*. The implications of the French Revolution, of the ideas of liberty, equality, fraternity and progress, of the change-over from the concept of subject to that of citizen, are not yet exhausted. Hence nationalism is not yet exhausted.

In fact, nationalism has gained new force, especially in underdeveloped countries, from the centralising, étatist consequences of the Industrial Revolution, from the vigorous emergence of the state as the regulator, protector and bearer of economic interests. To the nineteenth century, nationhood and independence were the necessary foundations of political progress; to the twentieth, they are also the necessary foundations of social and economic progress. Perhaps the first nationalist revolution in which the fusion of nationalism and the ideal of social and economic progress became clearly evident was the Mexican revolution, which was both nationalist and socialist. Since then, in a whole series of underdeveloped countries, political nationalism and the desire for progress have become almost inextricably interwoven.

## V

We are now in a position to see why I have been reluctant to begin, or even to end, this paper with a 'definition' of nationalism. *Eadem sed aliter* is the motto of history and of society. Concepts like 'nationalism' express and act as ideologies; they hold together disparate, logically separable, beliefs and attitudes, weld them into a unity, often by reference to something outside themselves. Nationalism, even modern political nationalism, is thus a complex phenomenon, which will contain elements of varying degrees of generality and specificity. We will find in it comparatively general atemporal elements, such as in-group loyalty, xenophobia, insecurities *vis-à-vis* a more powerful and impressive culture, the will to power and domination, etc., though each of those will be associated with specific, temporal material. We will find in it comparatively specific characteristics that spring from the culture of an epoch or a more widespread geographical area. We will also find even more specifically local concerns, in both the geographical and the temporal sense: the fear of socialists, or of Germans, or Jews, of the Papacy or the heretics. We cannot understand the difference between the Jewish rebellion against the Romans and the Indonesian rebellion against the Dutch, between the 'nationalism' of Bar Kochba and the nationalism of Sukarno, I believe, without reference to the organising middle tier of specifically modern conceptions presupposed and incorporated by modern political nationalism − the concepts of democracy, the political and social progress and, more recently, of the modernising power of the state. Yet the Chinese, the Zionist and the Indonesian of today does and can find inspiration in the culture, social organisation and heroic deeds of his forebears. He can do so, I believe, only temporarily − the backward-looking element in nationalism is even more transitional than that nationalism itself, and the nationalism that looks only backward has no social or political future. This, I believe, has become evident in the nationalisms that succeed in creating nation-states. It is so far less evident in a very new type of quasi-nationalism, that of the racial minorities in modern Western societies. The Australian Aboriginal's demand for land rights, the attempted elevation or restoration of tribal councils, the resurrection of the Black American's African heritage − these are not constitutions for the Aboriginal, Red Indian or Black American future. They are attempts to counterpose the dignity of the past to the insecurity of the present and to derive from that past a dignity and self-confidence with which to face the future. They are by their very nature narrowly transitional, attempts to create psychological preconditions for social, political and economic improvement. For the last two centuries, the nation-state has seemed the most obvious and direct path to such improvement and minorities have either assimilated or become socially invisible if not killed or expelled. Political nationalism has been intimately linked with that process. The importance of this nationalism is threatened only by its success. The problem of racial minorities in advanced democratic industrial societies, in securely established nation-states, may now take its place or, at least, for a period attract more public attention. Such minorities are too weak to create their own nation-states. For the moment they have turned, in the light of ever more rapid communication, to a certain pan-nationalism to bolster their confidence and help create a feeling of dignity. But they are, so far, parasitic upon the nation-state and its achievements: they seek its bounty or its protection. Where the host nation-state is not yet secure − in South Africa, Uganda, Malaysia, Burma, etc. − the 'national' or pan-national aspirations of minorities gain very short shrift indeed.

To say this, to insist that nationalism as a *general* phenomenon of outstanding importance in the modern world is best understood in relation to the conception of political and social and economic progress inaugurated by the French and the Industrial Revolutions, is not to say that the nature or significance of nationalism is exhausted by such an account. No one will be tempted to think that after reading the remaining contributions in this volume, contributions that bring out the extraordinary variety of material that can be caught up in nationalist ideology, the complexity of the functions it can serve, the peculiarity of the 'feel' as we confront it in specific contexts and specific societies. But I do believe that the particular character and role of each of these nationalisms — different as they are in so many respects — is not best understood by looking for a common definitive ingredient that is not tied to any particular time or place. It is much better grasped by examining it, initially, in the light of those fundamental and increasingly pervasive modern trends which give modern political nationalism a universal social significance. These trends, as I think all of the papers show, help to explain the character of such nationalisms even when they appear, as they did in Nazi Germany, as *prima facie* reactions against *modern* society, as attempts to escape from freedom into the emotional securities of the *Gemeinschaft* of kinship, locality and hierarchy, that is of blood, soil and the *Führerprinzip*.

**2**

# Two types
# of Nationalism

## *John Plamenatz*

Writers about nationalism mostly agree that there was little or none of it in the world until the end of the eighteenth century. They may not agree about how it is to be described or explained, and their attitudes to it range from strong condemnation to warm sympathy. But they speak of it as something essentially modern.

I shall not dispute this verdict, nor the widely held belief that nationalism arises in social conditions which also give rise to democratic and liberal ideas, even though it often takes illiberal and undemocratic forms. In the last century Acton attacked it as a danger, not only to order, but to liberty as well, and in this century it has been denounced as a perversion of democracy. These judgments are harsh and misleading, and are at best only half-truths. But I shall not dispute them either. I shall confine myself to arguing that nationalism, a phenomenon peculiar to peoples who share a cosmopolitan and secular culture in which the belief in progress is strong, has taken two markedly different forms. One form I shall call western and the other eastern. I do not suggest that the nationalism of every people falls clearly into one or other of these two categories. Nor do I deny that there are other ways of distinguishing types of nationalism just as important as this one. For this distinction I would claim only that it points to important differences that deserve more notice than they have received.

What I call eastern nationalism has flourished among the Slavs as well as in Africa and Asia, and is to be found also in Latin America. So I could not call it non-European, and have thought it best to call it eastern because it first appeared to the east of Western Europe.

Nationalism, as I shall speak of it, is the desire to preserve or enhance a people's national or cultural identity when that identity is threatened, or the desire to transform or even create it where it is felt to be inadequate or lacking. I say *national* or *cultural,* for what distinguishes a people from other peoples in their own eyes consists of ways of thinking, feeling and behaving which are, or which they believe to be, peculiar to them. Thus nationalism is primarily a cultural phenomenon, though it can, and often does, take a political form. It is related to, but different from, both patriotism and national consciousness.

Patriotism, or devotion to the community one belongs to, has existed for as long as there have been communities. Though the word was seldom used before the eighteenth century, the thing itself was old and familiar under other names, such as 'love of country' or 'loyalty to one's own people'. And national consciousness is only a lively sense of, and perhaps also a pride in, what distinguishes one's own from other peoples. It is a sense of cultural identity. It was as strong among the Greeks, the Romans and the Italians of the Renaissance as it has been anywhere in the last two centuries. But these three peoples were free of nationalism because they felt no need to preserve a threatened culture, even though two of them, the Greeks in the early years of the fifth century B.C. and the Italians in the sixteenth century, had to deal with foreign invaders. But the invaders were, in their eyes, barbarians; they were a threat to the independence of Greek and Italian cities rather than to Greek or Italian culture. Nationalism, as distinct from mere national consciousness, arises when peoples are aware, not only of cultural diversity, but of cultural change and share some idea of progress which moves them to compare their own achievements and capacities with those of others.

Perhaps I can make clear what I take nationalism to be, if I compare briefly the ideas of two writers, Rousseau and Herder, both of whom have been called forerunners of nationalism. There is more of nationalism, so it seems to me, in the pages of Herder than in those of Rousseau.

To be sure, Rousseau's idea of the state, of the independent political community, is quite different from that of earlier writers, such as Locke or Hobbes. He does not think of the citizens of a state merely as subjects of the same sovereign, for that would be compatible with the greatest cultural diversity. He insists that the people who make up an independent political community should have much the same customs and manners and much the same social ideals. In the *Considerations on the Government of Poland,* he advises the Poles to shorten the frontiers of their country, so that there should be only Poles inside it. But his real concern is always for the cohesiveness of the community and the quality of political life inside it. The equality and the moral freedom so precious to him can, he thinks, be achieved only in a community whose members feel an intense loyalty to it, which they will not do if their manners and values diverge greatly. That man is not born rational and moral, and becomes so only in the process of learning to live with others, to be a social being, was as clear to Rousseau as to any thinker of his own or the next century. But he rejected the faith in progress shared by so many of his contemporaries and saw no particular virtue in preserving a culture merely because it is distinct. There is no trace of political nationalism in his writings. He argues only that members of a political community, if that community is to be united and strong, must share the same fundamental values. He does not argue that people who share the same culture should be united in one political community the better to preserve it.

Herder was not a political nationalist either;[1] he did not aspire to the union of all Germans in one state. But he was concerned that whatever makes the Germans, or any people, culturally distinct from other peoples, whatever they cherish as peculiarly their own, should be preserved and developed. He cared for what made the Germans recognise one another as Germans, though some of them were Protestants and others Catholics, some subjects of the Hohenzollern and others of the Habsburg or of lesser sovereign princes. If he resented the cultural dominance of the French, it was because he thought it a threat to German culture, to the German spirit, to German customs and manners, ways of thinking and feeling. It did not occur to him that the preservation or development of that culture required the union of the Germans in one state. He disliked the Prussian state of his day, not because it was multinational and included Slavs and Jews as well as Germans, but because he thought it despotic and what we should today call bureaucratic.

Later, after his time, nationalism, even in the West, became intensely political. This was a result, largely, of the military and political ascendancy of the French under Napoleon. The French were formidable, were able to impose themselves on others, because they had a powerful state, and if other peoples were to preserve their independence or to resist excessive French influence, they too needed to form powerful states. In the circumstances, it was inevitable that nationalism should become political. Nevertheless, even in the West, it has always been primarily a cultural phenomenon, a desire to preserve or enhance a sense of cultural distinctness. It is this, above all, that distinguishes it from mere national consciousness.

In the fifteenth century, in the last stages of the Hundred Years' War,

---

[1] *Ideen zur Philosophie der Geschichte der Menschheit; Briefe zur Beförderung der Humanität.*

there was, among both the English and the French, a heightened national consciousness. Joan of Arc was not a legitimist; she did not fight for the Valois Charles VII against the Plantagenet Henry VI merely because she thought he had a better title to the French throne. She wanted to drive the English out of France. And the English at that time already saw themselves as conquerors of a foreign country, and boasted of their superiority over the French. But nobody in France was concerned to preserve French customs and ways of life, not to speak of the French language, against English influences felt to be excessive. There was no danger in the fifteenth century that France would be anglicised, and nobody thought of such a danger.

But the Germans in the latter part of the eighteenth century, even before the French invaded their country, even at a time when the victories of Frederick the Great were of recent memory and Napoleon had not yet been heard of, felt themselves threatened or at least overshadowed culturally by the French. They felt the need to assert themselves against the French. Even Herder, whose sympathies were wide and who disliked the Germanising policies of Joseph II in the non-German provinces subject to the Habsburgs, could not refrain from disparagement of things French. French ideas were a powerful influence in Germany both before the revolution and after it.

I say French ideas, although they were not so much French as West European. They were ideas about man, morals and society which had found expression as much in England as in France. They might even be called more English than French in so far as, at least until the time of the revolution, institutions and manners were more in keeping with them in England than in France. But their origins, social and intellectual, were West European generally. And the belief in progress, more and more widely accepted among the educated classes in the West, was defined by reference to them. Thus, it was not so much that English and French ideas were propagated chiefly by the French as that the English and the French were, for a variety of social and political reasons, better placed than other Western nations to elaborate upon these ideas and to apply them. During the period when belief in progress was fast catching on in the West, they were, or appeared to be, the pre-eminently progressive peoples. Among them national consciousness, as distinct from nationalism, was highly developed, and their two states were the most powerful in a part of the world which had already learned to think of itself as ahead of all the others. They were, inside the comity of nations that formed a consciously progressive civilisation, the pace makers, culturally, economically and politically. They were envied and admired. And if the French provoked more resentment than the English, it was probably because they were closer geographically to the other nations and more aggressive politically, as well as more conspicuously dominant culturally.

II

Thus nationalism is a reaction of peoples who feel culturally at a disadvantage. Not any reaction that comes of a sense of weakness or insecurity but a reaction when certain conditions hold. Where there are several peoples in close contact with one another and yet conscious of their separateness, and these peoples share the same ideals and the same conception of progress, and some of them are, or feel themselves to be, less well placed than others to achieve these ideals and make progress, nationalism is apt to flourish. This is not to set it down as merely a kind of envy. It is to suggest, rather, that it is to be found only among peoples who are, or are coming to be, sharers in an international culture whose goals are worldly. Nationalism is confined to peoples who, despite their rivalries and the cultural differences between them, already belong to, or are being drawn into, a family of nations which all aspire to make progress in roughly the same directions.

This, I suggest, is what we must take nationalism to be, if we assume (as most writers about it seem to do) that there was little or none of it in the West before the end of the eighteenth century. In that case, it is different from patriotism and national consciousness, which are both much older. And it is broader than the demand (or doctrine) that every nationally conscious people should form a state of their own or at least an autonomous province in a federal state. It is broader than merely political nationalism.

Critics of nationalism often speak of it as if it were essentially illiberal. Acton did so in the last century, and Kedourie has done so in this. For my part, I must say that what seems obvious to them does not seem so to me. No doubt, nationalists have quite often not been liberals, but that, I suggest, is largely because they have so often been active in conditions unpropitious to freedom, as the liberal understands it. I see no logical repugnance between nationalism and liberalism. Nationalists have been liberal and also illiberal, according to the circumstances in which they have found themselves.

There is nothing illiberal about cultural nationalism as such. Herder put a higher value on both individuality and cultural diversity, and claimed to see a connection between them. A human being becomes an individual, a rational and a moral person capable of thinking and acting for himself, in the process of acquiring the language and the culture of his people. He becomes a person distinct from others, in his own eyes and in theirs, by developing potentialities which can only be developed in assimilating a culture and learning to belong to a community. Diversity is desirable as much within the nation as between nations if the life of the individual is to be enriched. Herder respected the culture of the illiterate, of peoples and classes held to be uneducated because they lack the skills that bring power and wealth to their possessors. He also sympathised with the Jews in their desire to pursue their communal identity among hostile populations, and with the Slav peoples dominated culturally by the Germans. Peoples ought neither to cut themselves off from one another nor allow themselves to be submerged or absorbed. They should preserve and develop their peculiar inheritance, borrowing from others but not becoming mere imitators of them and so spiritually impoverished. For what impoverishes any people impoverishes mankind.

Such doctrines as these, looked at more closely, may turn out to be more elusive, more difficult to apply, than they appear at first sight. Nationalism, even at its best, is not the most perspicuous of creeds, if only because the criteria of national identity are not easily defined. But at least these doctrines are not illiberal. On the contrary, they are generous and tolerant.

Cultural nationalism can pass easily into political nationalism. It was to a considerable extent the power of the French state that lent prestige to the French language and to French ideas and manners in the seventeenth and eighteenth centuries. And the other people whose influence increased enormously during that period, the English, were also united in a powerful state. Thus, given cultural nationalism and the prestige and example of France and England, and given also the need for more efficient administration on a larger scale, it was only to be expected that such peoples as the Germans and the Italians should aspire to union within the frontiers of a national state so as to put themselves on a level with the English and the French.

As good an example as any of the political nationalist in the West is Mazzini.[1] Less learned, perhaps, than Herder, he was just as much a cultural nationalist and a champion of cultural diversity. He believed that all peoples have their own unique contribution to make to civilisation; they must therefore foster and develop whatever makes them distinctively the people they are. And they must respect in other peoples what they claim for themselves. In the economic and political conditions of the nineteenth century, if the Germans and the Italians, and other peoples placed as they are, are to make the best of their unique

---

[1] G. Mazzini, *Essays*, trans. Okey, London, 1894; *Selected Writings*, ed. N. Gangulee, London, 1946; *The Duties of Man and Other Essays*, London, 1955.

contributions, they too, like the French and the English, must be politically united.

This idea of unique contributions to civilisation by different nations implies that these nations are sharers in this civilisation, that there is a culture common to them all as well as cultures peculiar to each of them. This shared culture, which they enrich by their efforts, is presumably not unchanging, and to say that their efforts are (or can be) enrichments of it is to imply that it is progressive. Their efforts, their contributions, are assessed, presumably, by standards which form part of the common culture. The individual, in developing his capacities, appropriates a cultural inheritance which is more than merely national. But he cannot appropriate what is more than national without at the same time appropriating what is national. He cannot become a European unless he becomes an Italian or a German or a member of some other among the nations of Europe. But if he has a feeling of inferiority or inadequacy in belonging to whatever nation is his, he is unlikely to be as good a European as otherwise he might be.

Nationalism in the West in the last century, the first century of its real importance, though it was not entirely liberal, was so more often than not. It was so among the Germans and the Italians while they still aspired to political union and had not yet achieved it. In the next century, the twentieth, it has been much more often stridently illiberal, as it was in Fascist Italy, Nazi Germany and among extreme Right Wing groups in France. But in the West this illiberal nationalism has been the nationalism of peoples defeated in war or disappointed in victory. It has been the nationalism of peoples already united politically and humiliated or disregarded in spite of this unity.

### III

The Germans and the Italians, when they first became strongly nationalist, were already, by reference to standards they shared with the nations with whom they compared themselves, well equipped culturally. They had languages adapted to the needs, practical and intellectual, of the consciously progressive civilisation to which they belonged. They had universities and schools imparting the skills prized in that civilisation. They had, or had had, philosophers, scientists, artists and poets of European (or as they often put it) 'world' reputation. They had legal, medical, and other professions with high professional standards. They were therefore relatively well provided with the qualities and skills valued and admired by the Western peoples generally. To put themselves on a level with the English and the French, they had little need to equip themselves culturally by appropriating what was alien to them. Or, rather, culturally, they had (or until recently had had) as much to give as to take. Their most urgent need, so it seemed to them, was to acquire national states of their own, rather than to acquire the ideas and skills needed to run such a state, for they possessed them already in large measure.

The case with the Slavs, and later with the Africans and the Asians, has been quite different. Drawn gradually, as a result of the diffusion among them of western ideas and practices, into a civilisation alien to them, they have had to re-equip themselves culturally, to transform themselves. In their efforts to assert themselves as equals in a civilisation not of their own making, they have had, as it were, to make themselves anew, to create national identities for themselves. No doubt they already had some sense of identity or separateness when nationalism first began to take root among them. But there was an awareness also that the skills, ideas and customs acquired from their ancestors were inadequate, if they were to raise themselves to the level of the peoples who, by the standards of the civilisation into which they were being drawn, were more advanced than they were. This has made their nationalism in some ways profoundly different from that of the Germans, the Italians and other western peoples.

I shall speak now mostly of the Slavs because I happen to know more about them than about the peoples of Africa and Asia. But I believe that much of what I say about the Slavs applies also to these other peoples.

Nationalism came to the Slavs from the Germans. The interest in folkways and folklore which developed in Germany towards the end of the eighteenth century affected Bohemia, a partly German province. The first scholars to study Czech folklore and the Czech language were Germans: Nicholas Voigt, Dobner, Pelzel. The Czech scholars, Dobrowsky, Palacky and others, came afterwards; and the same is true of neighbouring Slovakia. Obradovic, who flourished in the last decades of the eighteenth century, was the first Serb to attach more importance to community of language and culture than to community of religion. But the Serbs of his day had no literary language; they had only a variety of spoken dialects. The only books in a Slav language circulating among them were in Church Slavonic, which was no more their language than it was the language of the Bulgars and Russians, or than Latin was the language of the Catholic peoples.

Serbo-Croatian, as it is written and spoken today in Yugoslavia, is largely the creation of philologists and grammarians who studied abroad, mostly in Vienna. So too Czech, Slovak and Slovene, as they are now used, are the creations of scholars who wished their peoples to have linguistic resources of their own greater than they already had. These new literary languages were, of course, created out of the old dialects. They are not like Esperanto. And yet they differ considerably from the old dialects in both grammar and syntax and, above all, in vocabulary. They meet needs, social, political and cultural, unknown to the peasant communities using the old dialects.

These Slav linguists and grammarians had two purposes in mind. They wanted to preserve for their people their own folklore to record and explain what was peculiar to them; and also to provide them with resources in their mother tongues which until then they had lacked. These two purposes were not, in their eyes, inconsistent with one another. If the Slav peoples took no pride in what they inherited from their ancestors, they might soon cease to be Slavs as they were drawn into a civilisation alien to them; and if they acquired no languages of their own adapted to the needs of that civilisation, they could not raise themselves to the level of the advanced peoples. These new languages would serve to draw together communities speaking a wide variety of dialects, thus enhancing their sense that they were one people, and would also enable them to acquire western ideas and practices.

The Slavs, if they were to become scientists or scholars or state officials or engineers, or anything else calling for skills and ideas other than those of peasants, had either to acquire a foreign language with resources different from those of their native tongues, or they had to be provided with Slav languages having these resources. If they learned a foreign language well enough for it to be the language of their work, of their profession, they were in danger of ceasing to be Slavs. If they acquired a Slav language having the same resources as German or French, a language into which German and French books could be translated, they risked losing touch with the folk cultures of their ancestors. They could, of course, continue to take an interest in them, but that interest would become increasingly scholarly and antiquarian rather than bound up with practical needs. To retain their nationality, their separate cultural identity, they had in many ways to imitate the foreigners with whom they refused to identify themselves. And in so doing they could not help but loosen the hold over themselves of ancestral ways. They might do it with regret, or eagerly and boldly, but they could not help but do it.

In the seventeenth and eighteenth centuries, as the Habsburg lands acquired a more centralised administration, and as industry and trade grew, large numbers of Slavs had become Germans. To make a career, to rise socially and acquire wealth, to live in the towns, they had to learn German and to become, to all intents and purposes, Germans. This process of Germanisation went on into the nineteenth century and may even have been accelerated, and there was added to it an extensive process of Magyarisation. But there was also in the nineteenth century, as there had not been earlier, a powerful resistance to these processes.

Why did people who in the past had been willing to pay the price of Germanisation in order to rise socially, in order to make careers, become unwilling to pay this price in the nineteenth century?

One answer is that, in the meantime, nationalist doctrines had spread from the German into the neighbouring Slav lands. The idea was spreading fast that it is important for a people to maintain their cultural identity, 'to be true to themselves', to 'follow their native genius' and not to allow foreign ways to seduce them from it – on pain of sterility and second-rateness if they did otherwise.

But what made this doctrine attractive? I suggest that the key to understanding nationalism in the Slav regions of the Habsburg Empire (and perhaps also in other parts of the non-Western world) is this: there was on foot a great social revolution turning societies in which the tightly-knit, tradition-bound and self-supporting village is the most important community into urbanised societies, with extensive trade, much greater social mobility, and a need for more complicated and centralised types of administration. This revolution had, of course, gone much further in the West. But in the Habsburg lands it was happening under the leadership of peoples having languages and cultures relatively well suited to new forms of activity at the expense of peoples who lacked them. There thus arose, within the Habsburg Empire, something analogous to the imperialism resulting from European penetration into Asia and Africa.[1]

The transformation of the first type of society into the second creates opportunities for the individual. He moves from the village into the town to make his fortune in trade or industry, or in one or other of the professions, or in the service of the state. This requires him to give up village ways and skills and village speech in favour of the speech and the ways and skills of those who have succeeded, who have risen socially, or who have long been on top. If he can do this easily, or can see no other way of achieving his ambitions, he does it; he pays the price. But if he sees himself at a great disadvantage, and has hopes of removing the disadvantage by combining with others who also suffer from it, he does combine with them. He refuses to pay the price of success required by those at the top, and demands that the price be different – less to his disadvantage.

As the social revolution gathers speed, as the number of people wanting to take the opportunities it creates grows rapidly, competition

[1] See O. Jaszi, *The Dissolution of the Habsburg Monarchy*, Chicago, 1929.

becomes fiercer, and the competitors less well placed to achieve success are keen to be as well placed as the others. If they are at a disadvantage because the language and culture of their ancestors are not well suited to the new opportunities, and if they are less well placed than others are to acquire the alien culture better suited to them, or if having acquired it their ancestry still counts against them, it becomes their interest to acquire a culture of their own as well suited to these opportunities as the alien culture. But this new culture cannot help but be in many ways an imitation of the alien one.

Nationalism of the eastern kind is both imitative and competitive. It arises in a world where social mobility and trade and a cosmopolitan culture are growing fast, where much the same standards, much the same ambitions are taking root everywhere, or at least over large areas, and yet some peoples are culturally better equipped than others are to live well by those standards and achieve those ambitions. And it arises as much among sophisticated as unsophisticated peoples.

The Chinese, while they merely despised foreigners, resented their intrusions and wanted to be rid of them, were not nationalists. They were then, so it is said, convinced of their superiority to foreigners. They had a high sense of what made them different and (in their own eyes) better than others. The proud and self-centred Chinese became nationalists only as they came to feel themselves at a disadvantage against the foreigners, as they came to doubt their superiority and to feel the need to prove to foreigners that they were as good as the foreigners were by cosmopolitan standards until recently quite alien to the Chinese. The Chinese seem now to feel this need strongly, and are busy transforming their country and making it different from what it was when they were so sure of their superiority. In transforming it, they may not be imitating either the West or the Soviet Union in all things, but they are imitating them in many. They admit that, in some ways, they are still backward. But if they are backward, it is not by their own standards of years ago; it is by standards they have come to accept quite recently, which they have not formed for themselves but have taken over from others.

Thus we have two kinds of nationalism. We have the nationalism of peoples who for some reason feel themselves at a disadvantage but who are nevertheless culturally equipped in ways that favour success and excellence measured by standards which are widely accepted and fast spreading, and which first arose among them and other peoples culturally akin to them. This is the nationalism of the Germans and Italians in the last century, the nationalism that I call western.

We have also the nationalism of peoples recently drawn into

civilisation hitherto alien to them, and whose ancestral cultures are not adapted to success and excellence by these cosmopolitan and increasingly dominant standards. This is the nationalism of peoples who feel the need to transform themselves, and in so doing to raise themselves; of peoples who come to be called 'backward', and who would not be nationalists of this kind unless they both recognised this backwardness and wanted to overcome it.

These peoples differ greatly from one another. Some are relatively primitive and mostly illiterate, as the Balkan Slavs were at the end of the eighteenth century, and as some African peoples still are. Others, like the Chinese and the Indians, were highly sophisticated long before they became nationalist and 'progressive'. Or at least their educated classes were so. Indeed, nationalism may have made them in some ways cruder and more stridently assertive than they used to be. They have lacked, not cultural diversity and sophistication, but merely the linguistic resources and other skills or dispositions favourable to success and excellence by cosmopolitan standards hitherto alien to them.

## IV

This 'eastern' nationalism is in some ways far removed from the spirit of Herder. It is both imitative and hostile to the models it imitates, and is apt to be illiberal.

But to pass these judgments on it without qualification is misleading. In practice there is no alternative to extensive imitation. The weaker and poorer, the unwesternised, peoples could not have cut themselves off from outside influences. The largest of them, the Chinese, tried to do just this, and failed. These peoples have all been either invaded or intruded upon; they have had to choose between submission and imitation, and they have chosen to imitate. It was the only way to assert themselves against the intruders; and it has involved both acceptance (imitation) and rejection (the demand for independence and the claim to be innovating as well as imitating).

It has involved, in fact, two rejections, both of them ambivalent: rejection of the alien intruder and dominator who is nevertheless to be imitated and surpassed by his own standards, and rejection of ancestral ways which are seen as obstacles to progress and yet also cherished as marks of identity.

Herder preached, not imitation, but respect for what is native. First absorb what your own people have to give you, and you will be better placed to appreciate what comes from abroad and to profit from it. Do not imitate the foreigner and do not reject him. Learn from him and let him learn from you, as befits equals. The Germans have at least as much to give to the French as the French to the Germans.

But this advice, which made excellent sense to the Germans at the end of the eighteenth century, makes rather less sense nowadays to the Chinese. Not because the native culture of the Chinese is poorer or more primitive than that of the Germans but because it is now of little help to the Chinese in their need to show that they are as good as (or indeed better than) the peoples who have treated them as inferiors.

Of course, peoples do not reject their native cultures completely; they do not even try to, and to the extent that they do try, they succeed only in part. Old ways of thinking and feeling persist even in the minds of the radicals and revolutionaries who think of themselves as deliberately breaking with the past. So, too, no imitation of foreigners ever makes the imitators quite like what they imitate. Nevertheless, the desperate attempt to 'catch up' with others, and therefore to imitate them extensively, in order to assert yourself against them by finding your own unique place in what has hitherto been their world, their civilisation, is profoundly disturbing. Eastern nationalism is disturbed and ambivalent as the nationalisms of Herder and Mazzini were not.

Eastern nationalism is also illiberal, not invariably but often. Leaders or rulers who take it upon themselves to create a nation or transform it, to provide it with skills, ideas and values it did not have before, are impatient of opposition. Their task, they think, is urgent, and they will not tolerate obstructive criticism, taking it for granted that it is for them to decide when it is obstructive.

Nevertheless, in some ways (important ways) their efforts are liberating. The new order they strive to establish offers new kinds of opportunity and destroys old types of authority. It gives to the individual a wider choice of occupations, and it weakens the hold of the family over him. He is usually freer than he was to marry whom he pleases. He is encouraged to be ambitious, to see himself as the maker of his own career, his own place in society. Though he is forbidden to criticise his rulers or the doctrines they propagate, he is introduced to science and to other kinds of rigorous and critical investigation. He learns that explanations vary, and that some are better than others. The very idea that men can deliberately change their ways of doing and thinking is liberating, even where the initiators of the change are harsh and oppressive.

Yet this nationalism, precisely because it is liberating, is also oppressive in new ways. The rulers of these new orders are sometimes called slave-drivers. If I say that this is to miscall them, it is not because I wish to defend them. Slaves are mere instruments, and those who drive them do not care what sort of persons they are, provided they do what they are told. But the nationalist ruler, oppressive though he may be, does care what sort of persons his subjects are. He may not care much about any particular person but he cares about the people generally. He wants to make a certain kind of community out of them. But a community is not made of people as a house is made of bricks. What makes it the kind of community it is, is that its members think and feel and behave as they do. The nationalist ruler wants his people to be as gifted and resourceful as the most advanced peoples. In his own eyes, he is more their leader than their master. He bullies them for what he thinks is their own good, and his idea of their good is that they should become responsible, alert and enterprising adults. These new rulers who demand so much of their peoples are in some ways more oppressive than the old rulers were, precisely because they try to reach deeper into their minds. But they see themselves as liberators and not oppressors, and their subjects to some extent accept them as such.

I have no wish to make light of the dangers of this type of nationalism. But it is not enough to point them out, as Western critics of nationalism so often do, and to express distaste for them. We must see this nationalism as part of a social, intellectual and moral revolution of which the aspirations to democracy and personal freedom are also products. It is connected with these aspirations, and even serves to strengthen them and to create some of the social conditions of their realisation, even though it so often also perverts them. In a world in which the strong and rich people have dominated and exploited the poor and the weak peoples, and in which autonomy is held to be a mark of dignity, of adequacy, of the capacity to live as befits human beings, in such a world this kind of nationalism is the inevitable reaction of the poor and the weak.

**3**

# Mass Politics
# and the Political
# Liturgy
# of Nationalism

**George L. Mosse**

The German historian Gottfried Gervinus wrote in 1852 that the
political movements of his time were supported by the instincts of the
masses. Gervinus was observing a phenomenon that was transforming
the politics of the age. Nationalism was a part of this transformation.
The rise of nationalism and the rise of mass politics joined hands during
the nineteenth century in Germany, where frustration with the outcome
of the wars of liberation against Napoleon coincided with the beginning
of modern mass politics. Nationalism became the principal movement
involving the people in the politics of their time.

Nationalism must be considered as linked to the democratic impulse
of the century, and it was this link which led to the creation of a new
kind of politics taking on liturgical form. The myths and symbols of
nationalism, its rites, monuments and festivals, appealed to the longings
of a multitude of people, and by drawing them into their orbit transformed a random mass into a cohesive and sometimes disciplined mass
movement. A new style of politics evolved, based upon a secularised
theology and its liturgy; democracy meant participation in the drama
which grew from these foundations. Such a theology determined the
self-representation of the nation, the way in which the people objecti-
fied their general will. This secularised religion developed throughout
the nineteenth century until the crowd became a disciplined mass acting
out the political liturgy, and this kind of political participation was
viewed by many as the true democracy. National Socialism was the
climax of this development, but it cannot be understood apart from the
long history of nationalism as a mass movement, based upon the shaping
of the crowd into a congregation.

We have recently been told that a new approach is needed to the
phenomenon of German nationalism, that we should explore the

relationship of this nationalism to practical reality, show less concern about culture and more about the economic aims of individual groups and the actual achievements and demands of nationalists. But the reality of nationalism, as it presented itself to most people and drew them into participation, was not economic nor defined through practical demands. Instead nationalism expressed itself through a new style of politics closely linked to a political theology. Such a political style has seemed vague and difficult to understand for those reared in the traditions of liberal or socialist thought. They continuously search for a logical political system and forget that men have been captured more often by theology than by the canons of classical political thought. Nationalism presented itself to its followers and became a reality to them through its liturgy. A liturgical drama defined the political aims of the movement and stood outside any sustained social, political or economic analysis. But, as nationalism also pioneered in taming the crowd into a mass movement, the new style of politics was destined to form the political reality of modern mass democracy, at least during the inter-war period.

It is from this point of view that we must consider several elements in the growth of the political liturgy of nationalism. A cultural fact remains fundamental to its growth: historical consciousness formed the basis of all modern nationalism. '. . . the best thing about history is', Goethe wrote, 'the enthusiasm it arouses'. Historical consciousness was awakened by myths expressed through symbols, but also through public festivals and national monuments. Rousseau had already advocated public cults as increasing man's virtues and deepening his love of the fatherland, and the French Revolution had put these cults into practice. Germans who advocated such festivals changed their thrust in an important manner; history and democracy must inform their ritual. Friedrich Ludwig Jahn, for example (1810), advocated the celebration of the past deeds of the people themselves and thought the battle of Merseburg in the early Middle Ages a particularly suitable memorial occasion, for here the peasants had defeated kings and bishops. Ernst Moritz Arndt's *German Society* (1814) had as its special task the celebration of 'holy festivals', partly pagan, such as the summer solstice, and partly recent, like the victory over Napoleon at the battle of Leipzig. He thought the festival to commemorate the noble dead in Germany's wars would be especially effective, for here 'history enters life and life itself becomes a part of history'.

But how was this to be accomplished? Arndt suggested a mixture of pagan and Christian symbolism. 'It is obvious that Christians begin festivals with quiet prayer and a pious Church service', but it was equally obvious that Germanic symbols like the oak leaf and the sacred flame must play their part. Arndt's ideas reflected actual practice. We know how the anniversary of the battle of Leipzig was celebrated throughout Germany in 1815. Men decorated themselves with oak leaves, made pilgrimages to fires on mountain tops or to pillars of fire lit on altars at street corners or in town squares. More often than not a priest or minister would preach before such an altar with the flame rising upon it, the 'altar of Germany's salvation' as it was often called.

This flame was a pagan symbol, connected with Freya the Goddess of Light and with the ancient festival of the summer solstice, which celebrated the triumph of light over darkness, of warmth and growth over the cold of night. It was also associated with the 'cleansing' of man's mind, with brotherly unity and an eternal ordering of life. But here, in 1815, it was placed on a Christian altar and the local minister stood in front of it. To be sure, the flame could also be associated with the eternal light which hangs over the altar in churches, but the celebration of the battle of Leipzig shows clearly the intermingling of secular and Christian elements in the national cult.

Their connection was not solely the actual church service. Patriotic festivals borrowed the liturgical rhythm of Protestantism, they stood close to the liturgical reforms which Friedrich Schleiermacher introduced into Protestantism during the 1820s and 1830s. Festivals would open and close with a hymn, there would be a confession of faith, a short sermon, and a dialogue between the speaker and the participants: the *responsa* of Christian liturgy. This borrowing was often quite deliberate, and it seems worthwhile to cite a later Nazi tract on festivals which asserted that the order of religious service must be kept intact, for it expresses a profound psychological truth through its principle of order. Moreover, such a service recognises the binding force of symbols as expressing the spirit of the community.

But this kind of order, which men like Jahn had also advocated, proved effective, at first, only among small groups. It was practised, for example, at the Wartburg festival of German student organisations (1817). But the ordering of larger masses proved a more difficult task. The first mass meeting in modern German history was probably the national festival at Hambach (1832), when 32,000 men and women gathered for a 'German May', the same month in which the ancient Germans had held their own *Thing*. The only truly organised part of the meeting was the procession up to Hambach castle in which flags and transparencies were carried, songs were sung, and the black, red and gold emblem worn.

Once at the castle, all was chaos and speeches; no liturgical form was attempted. The festival itself became a symbol but its actual proceedings could not be used as an example.

Instead, the liturgical cult of nationalism retreated into local celebrations and, above all, into the festivals of distinct groups like the male choirs, sharp-shooting associations and gymnasts. These latter, in particular, were associations concerned with the revival of national consciousness. By the 1860s their national festivals had acquired both order and form. The procession through the town was already elaborate and filled with national symbolism. But the festival itself contained unison singing and patriotic plays as well as speeches. The festival halls erected for the occasion held galleries where flags could be displayed, as well as a stage for choral representations. The sporting or shooting events took place separately from the patriotic part of these festivals. To be sure, the liturgy was not yet fully formed, and the emphasis upon the compulsory banquet and the beer-drenched socialising defeated the reverential atmosphere. Yet the crowd was no longer quite such a chaotic assembly as it had been at Hambach, though attendance ran into the tens of thousands. For one thing, among the gymnasts and sharp-shooters the wearing of a uniform was now compulsory, and even in 1817 the students had been asked to come to the Wartburg in Germanic costume with oak leaves in their caps. Cohesion through dress was not primarily linked to military examples.

But the real cohesion of the crowd was obtained through the space in which the festival took place. This was carefully arranged, often surrounded by towers and turrets, with the festival hall as a focal point, though in 1865 the sharp-shooters also used a giant Germania to accomplish this purpose. Space becomes all-important in the national cult, as indeed it was in the Christian religious service. As far back as the end of the eighteenth century Friedrich Gilly had designed a tomb for Frederick the Great, which was surrounded by a 'sacred space', containing monuments to other great Germans. Arndt had followed up this suggestion in surrounding his proposed monument to the battle of Leipzig with such a space, planted with oaks and serving as a war cemetery. But this 'sacred space' was to lose its association with the dead, becoming a cult space instead, where the national past came alive through action rather than in the contemplation of graves. The importance of such a sacred national space was clearly understood by the end of the nineteenth century.

By that time national monuments were designed with such spaces in mind, and in 1897, for example, various national monuments entered into bitter competition as to which of them should serve as the setting for national festivals. Clearly, such a fusion of symbol and festival was thought to determine the difference between a live and a dead national monument. Gymnasts, massed choirs and dance groups were to perform at such festivals. After 1918 the importance of liturgical space was further emphasised by mass movements, and especially National Socialism. 'The space which urges us to join the community of the *Volk* is of greater importance than the figure which is meant to represent the fatherland'. This is how the National Socialist art historian, Hubert Schrade, put it in a book on national monuments (1934). During the nineteenth century, national monuments or festival halls had formed a backdrop to the sacred space, but now the space itself comes to dominate the monument. The Tannenberg Denkmal (1925), erected to celebrate the German victory over the Russians in World War I provided the breakthrough, not consciously, but because the architects used the English Stonehenge as their model. They saw in this mysterious English monument an ancient Germanic meeting place. But this model served to produce a well-defined sacred space which was clearly distinct from the landscape which surrounded it. The monument centred upon a gigantic space surrounded by walls and eight towers; nearly 100,000 people could meet within its confines. Spatial considerations pushed the monument itself into the background. The liturgy had to be acted out by an ever-growing number of people.

The space was still sacred, it performed the same symbolic service as the national monument itself, as a self-representation of the nation. The surroundings of the monument were an integral part of the design. This included a 'sacred space', but the landscape within which it was set took priority. For, in this manner, the self-representation of the nation through stone and mortar was linked to the nation as symbolised in its eternal and unchanging landscape. Monuments like the famous Hermannsdenkmal (1836–75), built to commemorate the victory of Hermann or Arminius over the Roman legions, were set in natural surroundings filled with memories and remains of ancient German civilisation. For Wilhelm Kreis (1873–1955), a prolific builder and designer of such monuments, these were 'architectural mountains', the equivalent of the 'holy mountains' (like the *Kyffhäuser*), which played such an important part in national mythology. The natural setting will continue to play an important part in the design of sacred spaces, but the space itself becomes ever more important as the cult rite moves to the forefront, taking the place of the mere contemplation of static symbols.

The sacred space had to be filled by the liturgy. This grew both more elaborate and more systematic through the influence of new artistic forms which had not played a major part in its earlier formation. The discussion about the 'theatre of the future', which began in the 1880s, is important here, for it sought to unify dramatic action, fragmented by the arrangement of the conventional stage. An attempt was made to bridge the gap between actor and audience, stage and auditorium. Ancient models could be used, and Goethe had already seen in the ancient amphitheatre of Verona a device which united the masses and gave them a common spirit. The open-air theatre, where there was no scenery but only the surroundings of the German landscape, attained some popularity. Gottfried Keller had proposed such a theatre in 1859, where folk dances and male choirs would act out Germanic myths. After 1903 many such theatres came into being, always with a national purpose in mind. They were supposed to provide a vehicle for carrying the myth to the people, and the Nazis were to adopt them for their *Thing* theatres.

Richard Wagner's purpose was also to carry the *mythos* to the *Volk* and he saw his operas as deeds of national regeneration. His theory of the new theatre was explicit: reality must first be dissolved into a dream and through this dream the people would grasp the serious purpose of life. The unending dream of sacred *'völkisch'* revelation will return to them clearly and full of meaning. The living symbols of the stage must speak directly to the audience, and that is why he advocated the concealed orchestra, as well as the peculiar shape of the auditorium.

Wagner's theatre was meant as a setting for operas which were national festivals, and within which the liturgy could be acted out. No applause was permitted to disturb the cult reverence. The audience participated in the shared atmosphere, by taking part vicariously in the *mythos* which was acted out in front of them. But for a true national liturgy this was not good enough, for the audience must be drawn into active participation. Yet the 'new theatre' provided an important framework for the liturgy, through the creation of a shared atmosphere, within a clearly defined space, vital to any cult rite or to the formation of the masses. The sacred space below national monuments fused symbol and action, the new theatre created another kind of space for worship which tended to emphasise a shared contemplation. But this required a more elaborate acting-out of the liturgy and this, in turn, meant the adoption of certain artistic media which had been present earlier only in fragmentary form.

Speaking choruses and choral plays seemed suited to the new cult theatre. These were especially relevant to the dramatic in the liturgy.

Choral plays were in reality choirs of movement which fused musical and visual representation. The choirs sang and moved but also engaged in a dialogue with a single speaker, a kind of interchange between priest and congregation. This choral theatre 'no longer represents individual fate to the audience, but that which concerns the community, the *Volk* . . . Thus, in contrast to the bourgeois theatre, private persons are no longer represented but only types.' The mass theatre perforce led to stereotyping, though this had been inherent in all the symbols of nationalism.

Another device also became popular in order to draw actors and audience into a unity. Speaking choruses engaged in dialogue with the audience itself, an impressive ritual adapted from the Christian *responsa*, first popularised by the Communists, whose pioneering efforts the Nazis, who made full use of such choirs, gladly acknowledged. Rhythm played an important part in such theatre, just as rhythm was a crucial element in forming the crowd into a disciplined congregation. Such rhythm had been provided by the gymnasts earlier and by folk dances within the sacred space. But after 1918 the emphasis on rhythm was further extended. The military influence was present, but in the processions rather than in the actual ceremonial. Here the modern dance of the 1920s is of special interest.

Mary Wigman and all the founders of the modern dance stressed bodily movement and the space into which these movements were projected. Movement forms space. These movements were group movements, 'dancing choirs' which were thought most effective in organising space. The modern dance, then, was concerned with both movement and space: two factors always involved in organising the masses. The earlier national festivals like that of Hambach had been chaotic because they had been unable to form space and movement into a unity. The binding element of the modern dance was rhythm, but a preoccupation with lighting played a major role. Mary Wigman believed that the play of light was of equal importance with dance, music and rhythm in organising space.

The modern dance went hand in hand with the movement of rhythmic gymnastics so popular in the 1920s. These arts were put to practical use in the organisation of festivals by Rudolf von Laban who taught the organisers how to induce 'communal movement. . .festive walking and virile running'. These were supposed to conquer space.

The conquest of space by the masses was vital to any formation of the political liturgy. Ideally there should be no actors, only participants. But in reality it was the actors who became a mass — choral movements, group dancing. The lay plays performed by the German Youth Movement had their place here as well. For in these plays the amateur actors themselves formed a cohesive group and were thought to be representative of the people as a whole. Typically enough, these Youth Movement lay plays were morality plays and many of the dramas of modern dance were taken from the traditions of medieval morality plays as well. This conquest of space was designed to transmit a morality and a myth to the people, not dissimilar to Wagner's efforts. The conquest of space meant acting out a cult rite on behalf of the community. The word 'lay' in lay plays was given its ancient Germanic meaning of belonging to the *Volk*, to the community.

Artistic creativity was transformed into a cult rite. Individually these art forms remained confined to definite groups of devotees much smaller than the older associations of gymnasts, sharp-shooters or the male choral societies. The modern dance was not even nationalist in its perception. But these art forms provided some of the building-blocks for a fully-fledged national liturgy. They did so in opposition to the fossilisation of art, society and government during the Wilhelmian Reich. Then festivals seemed to have lost their impetus and degenerated into military parades, with the people as spectators on the sidelines. Wagner's Bayreuth, the new theatre and the other new art forms we have discussed were meant to break through this impasse.

To be sure, Bismarck himself was admired and, at times, loved as the founder of the Reich. But even under his rule an uneasy feeling prevailed that national unity lacked the spiritual cement needed to give it meaning and cohesion. The stepped-up tempo of industrialisation, rapid urbanisation and the spectre of class strife, undoubtedly increased this feeling. But it reached its climax when Bismarck was dropped by the young Emperor. William II loved posturing and operatic display, but he acted out his dramas abroad rather than at home.

National unity had come from above and not from below, it was the gift of statesmen and the democratic impulse seemed lost. This fact seemed to stifle the official national cult. While national unity had to be achieved against the establishment, the political liturgy of nationalism showed an ideological and dramatic impetus which was lost once nationalism had become established doctrine. But, as Jahn had already remarked, festivals could not be successful if they were simply decreed and manipulated from above. They had to be infused with spontaneity arising out of a democratic thrust based upon shared historical memories. The people must worship themselves and not a king or mere military power and glory.

Such democracy was basic to all this political liturgy and it meant, as we have seen, active participation by the people in myth and symbol. Wilhelmian nationalism itself seemed a dead rather than a live national monument, and indeed such monuments swamped the nation during this period leading, as one writer put it, only to boredom. Moreover, official festivals were closely tied to orthodox Protestantism. The minister did not preach German patriotism, standing before an altar with a pillar of flame upon it and almost forgetting to mention God or Christ in the process. Instead, he now preached a sterner gospel of loyalty to the government and the ascetic Christian virtues.

The revolt against such imposed national cults also gave new impetus to the separation of the national liturgy from Christianity. Already in the festivities of male choirs and sharp-shooters the Church was absent, perhaps because their members were both Protestant and Catholic. But now the political liturgy tended to claim autonomy, though this was never total and the basic pattern of borrowing remained intact. Yet the new devices for the organisation of the masses, which we have discussed, did not refer themselves to Christian examples, except perhaps in the content of their morality plays.

However, no clear separation took place until the Nazi era, and even then it was ambivalent. While in 1933 Joseph Goebbels still spoke of national ceremonies as cult acts paralleling those of Christianity, by 1938 Adolf Hitler insisted that a clear distinction be made between cults that were religious in nature and 'völkisch'-political teaching. This attempt to divide the Christian from the national cult was part of Hitler's battle against the churches.

If for the wider Nazi ceremonial the new ideas of liturgical space were adopted, this was not the case for more intimate liturgical rites and, at times, the buildings used for this purpose closely resembled the arrangements in a church. Thus a 'sacred chamber' in a factory retains the apse, the benches and even the confines of the altar. Hitler's own unpublished sketchbook for 1925 shows the design of a hall for national ceremonials which is reminiscent of a giant church. The famed rotunda, which was to be the centrepiece for the new Berlin, could not get away from church design. Yet Hitler was always careful that the buildings of the Nazi movement should dwarf the church towers near them. Obviously, in Nazi ceremonial, no priest or minister took part. Instead, together with the flag, the sacred flame assumed a central significance of its own: the flame of sacrifice. This might flicker from towers especially constructed for this purpose, as for example, when those who had died in the Hitler *Putsch* of 1923 were transferred to their final resting place at Munich's Feldherrnhalle.

Such towers gave great visibility to the flames, as the altars had done in 1815. But they also had the example of the Bismarck towers before them. These towers were constructed all over Germany at the turn of the century in order to commemorate the deeds of the Chancellor. They were supposed to imitate the monuments which the ancient Germans and Saxons had erected over the tombs of their heroes, and were crowned with a flame. National Socialism adopted secular symbols now supposedly cut off from those of Christianity. But even after the Nazi seizure of power, the Christian and the Nationalist could continue to exist in almost blasphemous proximity. The Christmas play performed in 1933 before the employees of the German railroads provides a good example. The play took place around a Christmas tree in the middle of the auditorium. The commentator drew a parallel with the Greek theatre. The struggle and victory of Christianity provided the theme: crusaders appeared, and mercenaries, the S.A. marched to the crib, with the swastika flying. Final victory is achieved in the end: 'God sent us a saviour at the moment of our deepest despair: our Führer and our wonderful S.A.' The film of the proceedings blends in Hitler's picture at this point, superimposed upon the Holy Family and the Christmas tree. The Christian and the National Socialist drama of salvation were united, German myth and symbol fused with those of Christianity. Moreover, the connection between Germanic and Christian myth was further strengthened when it was pointed out that Christ's birthday coincided with the winter solstice.

Quite obviously, it was felt that Christian tradition must be used to support the drama of salvation which grew out of a Germanic theology. But such a link, common at the beginning of the nineteenth century, was exceptional during the Third Reich. Yet the deeper connection between the Christian and national liturgy was always present, though secular symbols were in the forefront and the principles derived from the artistic development of the *fin de siècle* were adopted.

But these were not the only factors which contributed to this secularised religion. The workers' movement also provided examples which could be imitated. Two were of special importance: May Day and the use of flags. Both became linked, not to the actual acting out of the liturgy within the sacred space, but to the processions which opened and closed these ceremonies. Processions had always taken on a more fully disciplined form than the actual ritual, they were easier to keep coherent through the symbols they carried (and sometimes acted out as a play within the procession), through common dress or emblems worn by all. But the May Day parades impressed through their massiveness and they were supposed to be silent. The combination of tens of thousands marching with massed red flags and the deep silence that prevailed, symbolised concretely that 'we have the numbers, we are the masses, we have the power'. It is significant that Hitler designated as final, in a liturgical sense, the silent march to the memorial for the fallen heroes in the Luitpoldshain during the Nuremberg party rallies. The training camps of the Nazi teachers' organisation also ended their course with a silent torch-light parade to a lonely height or to a pillar of flame.

The massed flags carried on May Day, with their startling red colour (a colour which was borrowed for the Nazi flag itself), served as an example of how the 'entry' *(Aufmarsch)* into a hall should take place. The cult of the flag itself dates back to the beginning of the century but the preoccupation with the flag as a symbol reached its height during the *fin de siècle*. Then Theodor Herzl was fairly typical in the time he spent designing a flag for a non-existent nation, 'for with a flag one can do anything, even lead people into the promised land'. Herzl can also illustrate how deeply some men at that time felt the need for a political liturgy: 'only sounds, music and pictures can move the masses'.

The flag connected past and present, it provided a focal point for this symbolism, as it had been the focal point for armies earlier, providing a point of orientation for soldiers during battle. As a manual for Nazi party officials put it, the flag forms an indissoluble unity with that human being who carries it, fusing both into one historical continuity. The symbolism of the flag was similar to that of the sacred flame; both concretised historical consciousness. The cult of the flag was particularly associated with the blood of past heroes, it symbolised martyrdom for the sake of the nation. The flag stood for patriotic action. It is not without interest that the Nazis took over the 'song for the entry of the flags' from the First of May celebrations, substituting the ideal of the nation for world revolution.

The examples of the development of the liturgy which we have given should make clear its thrust and its nature. But a fully-formed liturgy also meant, as Hans Meyer has pointed out, that symbolism and ritual must be more important than the contents of speeches, that the speaker must become merely one part of the total *mise en scène*. This goal was never reached by the workers' movement which, for all its ceremonial, continued to stress didactic speech-making as the centre of its rite. Education of the masses through speeches was also part of the nationalist liturgy as it developed, but the educational function never dominated. From the very beginning speeches as part of the national rite had, in fact, been confessions of faith and as such fitted in easily with the surrounding symbols. The leader who made the speech continued to be of the greatest importance, his charisma was necessary to draw in the masses and to inspire them. But the symbols and universal participation were equally important within the whole setting, the 'sacred space'.

Gustave Le Bon influenced not only Hitler but many leaders of the nationalist Right in his analysis of the crowd. His contention, that the leader does not stand above the crowd but is part of the shared myth, proved undoubtedly correct. The Nazis instructed their sub-leaders to give only short speeches, recognising that they must fit into a total ceremonial. During one ceremony Hitler himself formed part of the marching crowd, emerging only at the end in order to give his speech.

Propaganda films, even when Hitler spoke, showed, with few exceptions, shots of the masses rather than of one individual. The speeches themselves were primarily declarations of faith, though they could also contain programmatic statements. They stood in the tradition of the Wartburg festival or other similar occasions which took place during the nineteenth century. Joseph Goebbels remarked that when Hitler spoke it was like a religious service. This could hardly be said of the speeches of most Socialists and Liberals. But the cult speeches of Adolf Hitler and his predecessors did form a unity with the atmosphere of worship which suffused the political liturgy.

Sole emphasis upon the leader has served to disguise the fact that totalitarianism was never a simple confrontation between leader and people but also needed mediating devices between the governors and the governed. The liturgy of nationalism was such a device in this case, replacing political participation through parliamentary government.

Hitler realised this clearly, for he designated certain ceremonies as a final liturgy and others as merely provisional. He held that it was the liturgy which would safeguard the future of the Third Reich. Whoever came after his death was bound to be mediocre, but within a fully-formed liturgy it would not greatly matter what sort of man the future *Führer* turned out to be; he was one symbol among others, a living focal point of the liturgy like the priest in a church.

This stress upon theology may seem odd in a world said to be dominated by pragmatic politics. But men from Arndt to Hitler sincerely believed that it would, in fact, make concerted political action possible. Parliamentary regimes did find it difficult to operate in an age of mass democracy, and they could never find a binding force strong enough to overcome political fragmentation. They tried to institute festivals but these, like Constitution Day in the Weimar Republic, proved a failure.

Any liturgy must provide a fully-furnished home and cannot be instituted on a partial basis; the world must not only be explained but a healthy world must take the place of the dilemma of modernity. That had been the appeal of Christianity for centuries, and it also had to provide the appeal for a political liturgy if it was to be successful.

This healthy world gave a positive cast to the liturgy of nationalism. The enemy was not represented in the symbols of festivals or on national monuments. He was present only in the speeches. Christian liturgy did contain references to sin as well as salvation, though the piety associated with Schleiermacher's reform of Protestantism minimised this aspect of Christianity. From the very beginning of nationalism, ideas of battle and struggle had been enveloped in a mythology which subordinated them to the concept of national regeneration. They were often an implicit rather than an explicit part of national self-representation.

Thus Hitler always inveighed against 'being negative', by which he meant that one should stress the positive element of regeneration inherent in the cult. Typically enough, the visual spread of Jewish stereotypes went on outside the official ceremonial of the Third Reich. Here the shared worship counted, the shared atmosphere and the organisation of the masses. Wagner, for example, had made a similar distinction between the enemy, the Jew, who filled many of his prose works and his 'national deed', his operas, from whom any portrayal of this enemy is absent. (Perhaps with the exception of Mime in the Nibelungen Ring cycle, who has sometimes been considered the stereotype of evil, and even of the Jew.)

This appeal from a sick to a healthy world always emphasised the 'beauty of holiness'. Perhaps this is one of the reasons why the ugly enemy is not allowed to appear. The action, symbols and monuments were bound together by an ideal of beauty which derived largely from Greek sources, and more specifically from the classical revival of the late eighteenth century. Beauty consists in true proportion which must encompass all variety. According to Johann Joachim Winckelmann, who set the tone for the subsequent definitions of the content of the beautiful (*History of Ancient Art*, 1764), a 'noble simplicity and quiet greatness' formed the ideal. Moreover, passion has no place in this beauty. To quote Winckelmann once more: sculpture must possess the unity of the surface of a sea which at some distance appears smooth and still, although constantly in movement.

This ideal of beauty would end man's alienation and reconcile him to the chaotic world. The function of beauty was clearly expressed by

Friedrich Theodor Vischer's *Aesthetics or the Science of the Beautiful*
(1846-57), a book which, as Heinrich von Treitschke aptly remarked,
was used by everyone even if it was not specifically acknowledged. The
function of beauty was to produce a healthy world beyond the confines of rational consciousness. It brought to light an ideal which was
within all men, and this expressed itself through a Greek ideal form.

To be sure, the Greek form became interlaced with elements of
romanticism, especially as national monuments had to be monumental
and impressive. A pyramidal construction was adopted in some cases, for
to the Romantics the pyramids represented both mystery and monu-
mentality. But even so, classical design remained clearly visible. The
Völkerschlachtdenkmal (Monument to the Battle of the Nations) at
Leipzig (1913) provides a good example of this mixture, and so does the
Shrine in Melbourne (1934), which transferred such symbolism in what
might be called its purest form to the Australian continent. Friedrich
Gilly, in the last years of the eighteenth century, had already superimposed a pyramid upon a classical temple as a form of national self-
representation. The idealisation of the landscape and symbols like the
sacred flame were romantic rather than classical; still their use was also
related to the noble simplicity and quiet greatness thought necessary
for the national cult. The Greek ideal of beauty is evident in all permanent monuments of national self-representation, as well as in the stereotype of the ideal German. But its concept of beauty also served to dis-
cipline the masses — not merely through the form of the Greek amphitheatre which inspired much of the 'theatre of the future', but also
through the principles of harmony, proportion, and the absence of
passion which might lead towards chaos. Hegel had already held, and
Vischer echoed him, that beauty must avoid any merely accidental
elements.

The liturgical forms with which we have been concerned received
their cohesion partly through their own rhythm and symbols, and
partly through the ideal of beauty which also formed them into a unity.
Again, the parallels with Christian liturgy are self-evident, and in the
last resort the appeal of this political style was the same as that of traditional western religion. But, in addition, this appeal also served to give
a cohesive form to the shapeless mass of adherents.

Moreover, the appeal of this liturgy was cross-class, and thus fulfilled a unifying function which socialism never achieved. The gymnasts,
the choral societies and the sharp-shooters all contained bourgeois and
working-class members. When, in the 1890s, the workers began to with-
draw from these organisations and to found their own sports, singing

and (to a lesser extent) shooting societies, the break was never complete. Indeed, more singers and gymnasts remained within the bourgeois organisations than joined the workers' clubs. The workers' organisations themselves aped the festivals of their bourgeois counterparts. Thus, for example, the workers' song festival of 1914 started with a procession to the march from Wagner's *Tannhäuser* and then passed on to a speech by Kurt Eisner. By 1925 their ever more elaborate procession started with representations of the ancient Germans, passed on to a blond Germania flanked by oaks, but ended with a Goddess of Freedom whose chariot was draped in the colours of the Weimar Republic. The Republic was anchored in Germanic myth. Similar examples could be provided from the ceremonial of the workers' sports association which was the largest Socialist movement during the Weimar Republic for, until 1927, it contained both Social Democrats and Communists.

The workers were drawn into the national movement through their own adoption of the nationalist liturgy, though this was always combined with Republican symbols and songs of freedom. Yet it seems that the cult component of nationalism cut across classes long before the Nazis used this tradition in a conscious manner. This seems a potent reality of nationalism.

The pragmatic side of the national cult must not be ignored. Some of the form it took sprang from the needs of the moment. When Albert Speer organised the great Nazi festival on the Tempelhoferfeld in 1934 he had to face the problem that the site was a flat air field — the airport of Berlin. The dimensions were vast and the stage had to be visible to everyone. For this reason he hit upon the use of huge over-dimensional flags bathed in light which set off the stage. These flags were to perform this function at all subsequent mass meetings. The famous dome of light over the field was invented not out of any past model, but because Speer had watched flack batteries in action. Yet his basic aim was the same as that which we have discussed, namely to create a clearly defined space, for the masses had to be contained and disciplined and a common mood had to be created. Pragmatic experiment fitted itself into the development of the national liturgy.

The nationalism we have discussed is only one facet of a complex movement and by no means all nationalists were captured by this theology and its liturgy. Certain social, economic and political conditions were necessary in order to activate this cult and to make it effective. The objective conditions, as Karl Marx called them, must always be kept in mind. Nevertheless, the national cult was central to the way in which nationalism presented itself to the people and involved them in its aims. For whatever the economic or social features of this movement, it operated in an age of mass politics, at a time when many other European political movements and ideologies ignored or deplored this development. The climax of nationalism as a political liturgy came with the advent of National Socialism. But it would be wrong to view this development solely in connection with the Third Reich, for it had a long history behind it and was applied in other nations as well.

Much of what has been analysed here would also hold true, for example, in Italy where first Gabriele D'Annunzio and then Benito Mussolini practised an identical political style. Perhaps such an approach to politics was especially relevant to newer nations who had not been united over a long period of time. It may well be significant that today Israel, rather than the European nations, remains involved with such symbols and myths. Here also a binding force had to be created in a new nation, and the Zionist leaders brought the liturgy with them from central and eastern Europe. However, it seems much more controversial to see this political liturgy operating as an integral part of modern mass society, though with a changed content. Maurice Edelman has argued persuasively that precisely this is the case in the United States. If so, then what we have discussed is not merely a part of nationalism but indeed has in some sense become the political style of mass politics and mass democracy.

Adolf Hitler told the Nuremberg rally of 1935 that history finds no nation really worthwhile unless it has built its monuments. He meant by this the political liturgy of nationalism as the only viable mass politics. Whether worthwhile or not, it did at one point in history provide the binding force for a mass movement which endured for over a century. The theory of nationalism never varied much over that span of time; it is the acting out of this theory as a secular religion which served to give nationalism the dynamic of victory.

**4**

# The Evolution of
a Myth —
The Easter Rising,
Dublin 1916

*F. X. Martin*

Augustine Birrell was that rare British official in Ireland — an Englishman who largely understood and sympathised with the people he was ruling. As chief secretary for Ireland, 1907-16, he was in effect the governor of the country. Particularly during his early years of office he travelled frequently throughout the land — in his own words, 'there never was any chief secretary so peripatetic as I was' — and he constantly asked himself the vital questions, 'What is the real Ireland, the new Ireland, the enfranchised Ireland, thinking about? Whitherwards is it tending?'[1] An indication of his sympathy was the liberal support he gave to the Irish language; it was a measure of his diplomacy and common sense that he succeeded in solving, at least provisionally, that most intractable of Irish problems, the university question, by founding the National University of Ireland. Yet, paradoxically, he was, in the witty phrase of a recent authority on the rising, 'the chief casualty of Easter Week'.[2]

## Birrell's judgment
Birrell may be excused for the hard feelings he held about the rising. It led immediately to his resignation, wrecked forever his political career, and due to it he felt 'personally . . . smashed to pieces'.[3] In his enforced retirement he remained urbane and tolerant on most issues, and even though he commented on the rising with unwonted asperity his considered judgment deserves attention:[4]

[1] A. Birrell, *Things Past Redress*, London, 1937, p. 212.

[2] Leon Ó Broin, 'Birrell, Nathan, and the men of Dublin Castle', in *Leaders and Men of the Easter Rising*, ed. F.X. Martin, London and Ithaca, 1967, p.13.

[3] Birrell, *Things Past Redress*, p. 221.

[4] Ibid., p. 219.

As a 'rebellion' it was a ridiculous failure from the first, but as an event in Irish history it was horrible and heartbreaking, and being accompanied by house-to-house fighting, sniping, and murdering, it stains the memory. It was a supreme act of criminal folly on the part of those who were responsible for it, for it never had a chance, and was really nothing more than a Dublin row.

These lines were not penned in the first chagrin of his resignation but were written twenty years later, in 1936, in the peace of his secluded home at Chelsea. Moreover, he had expressed the same opinion when writing to the Prime Minister, Asquith, on 30 April 1916, the day after Pearse signed the unconditional surrender:[5]

It is not an Irish rebellion – it would be a pity if *ex post facto* it became one, and was added to the long and melancholy list of Irish Rebellions.

Birrell, attuned to Irish traditions and the Irish mentality, was forewarning Asquith, while the centre of Dublin was still a smoking ruin, that the real danger was not the armed effort of the rebels (which he assessed realistically as a puny military demonstration) but its political consequences in terms of nationalist propaganda. He foresaw that the armed revolt in Dublin might well be invested with all the glamour of a national myth and rank in popular Irish estimation with the rebellions of 1641 and 1798.

Yet Birrell effectively undid his own advice when in the same letter of 30 April to Asquith he indignantly remarked, 'The leaders, both fighting leaders and stump-orators, are criminals, to whom short shrift should be given'.[6] Thus by a stroke of his own pen Birrell was inscribing the names of Pearse, Clarke, MacDermott, Connolly, MacDonagh, Ceannt and Plunkett, the seven signatories of the proclamation of the Irish Republic, at the end of that long list of 'martyrs, heroes and felons of our land' which ran from Art MacMurrough Kavanagh in the fourteenth century to O'Donovan Rossa in 1915. It was as Pearse and his companions had hoped and planned for. How still more indignant would Birrell have been had he realised that he was, all unwittingly, assuming a role in a play conceived by the extreme Irish nationalists and designed to create a further cycle in (what he would regard as) the national myth.

### The proclamation as a historical interpretation
When Pearse, bare-headed and dressed in his grey-green Volunteer

[5] Cited in Leon Ó Broin, *Dublin Castle and the 1916 Rising,* Dublin, 1966, p. 121.

[6] Ibid., p. 120.

uniform, stepped out in front of the General Post Office shortly after noon on Easter Monday to read the proclamation of the Irish Republic he was convinced that it was a supremely historic moment for the country, yet on this of all occasions his magnetism for once ebbed from him. He was pale-faced, tense, and the by-standers showed little appreciation of the great moment as he proclaimed a free Ireland. There were a few thin, perfunctory cheers; no enthusiasm, no hostility as yet. If at that moment the incandescent quality of Pearse's words kindled no fire in the listeners there was even less likelihood they would perceive that the document he was reading was not only a historic declaration but a historical interpretation of over seven hundred years of Irish history.

It began with the resonant assurance that the insurgents were acting in the name of God and of the dead generations of Irishmen; it went on to insist that England's long occupation had given it no right to the country, that in every generation the Irish people had rebelled against the usurpation of their rights, that there had been six rebellions during the previous three hundred years, and that these rights were now once more being affirmed by the soldiers of the Irish Republic. Here sonorously yet clearly expressed was what Birrell regarded as the greatest danger of the rising, the declaration that the insurgents acting in the names of Tone, Emmet, Davis, Mitchel and O'Donovan Rossa represented the political aspirations of an oppressed Irish people. At the very outset of the rising, therefore, the pitch was being queered for the historians. The proclamation of the republic was presenting them with an interpretation of the past in order to explain the present. It was also presenting young Irish nationalists with a program for the future.

## The rising of a drama

The weakness of the rising was ultimately its strength. It was imaginatively planned with artistic vision and with exceptional military incompetence. I have dealt elsewhere with the military aspect,[7] but the immediate object here is to consider the artistic image created by the rising since it was this which rightly alarmed Birrell.

The revolt was staged consciously as a drama by its principal actors. It is not without significance that Pearse, Plunkett and MacDonagh had all directed plays in their time – Pearse at St Enda's College, Plunkett and MacDonagh in the Hardwicke Hall. The theatrical element was noticeable in several of the leaders – MacDonagh with his sword-stick and cloak; Eamonn Ceannt with his kilt and bagpipes; Plunkett, with a

---

[7] F.X. Martin, 'The Easter Rising – a *coup d'état* or a bloody protest?', in *Studia Hibernica*, no. 8, 1968.

filigree bangle on his wrist and antique rings on his fingers, moving around the G.P.O. on inspection, a Mauser automatic pistol and military sabre dangling from his Sam Browne belt; Countess Markievicz, who had several times played on the stage, concluding her activities in Easter Week at the time of the surrender by ostentatiously kissing her revolver and Sam Browne belt as she handed them over to the British officer, Captain de Courcy Wheeler.

When Pearse founded St Enda's College at Cullenswood House in 1908 he had a saying of Cú Chulainn, the Irish hero of pre-historic times, emblazoned around a fresco where all the boys might see it — 'I care not though I were to live but one day and one night, if only my fame and my deeds live after me'. Pearse consciously prepared for the role of national martyr, composing for his mother that moving poem:

> THE MOTHER
> I do not grudge them: Lord, I do not grudge
> My two strong sons that I have seen go out
> To break their strength and die, they and a few,
> In bloody protest for a glorious thing,
> They shall be spoken of among their people
> The generations shall remember them,
> and call them blessed.

The leaders of the revolt saw themselves as inheritors of Ireland's tragic past, committed willy-nilly to violent action in order to arrest the attention of their complacent countrymen, but playing in fact for the benefit and applause of future generations of Irishmen. However unreal the play may have seemed beforehand, however disturbing the uncertainty which at times may have chilled the hearts of the more reflective of the conspirators during the months of preparation, there is no doubt that Pearse and his companions showed an unerring theatrical instinct in the *mise en scène,* in the roles they chose and the lines they spoke.

As a centrepiece for the drama the General Post Office was selected; it was a disastrous choice as a military headquarters but since it stood prominently on one side of the main thoroughfare of the city its seizure meant that not only would all normal activity in Dublin be disrupted but from it defiance would be trumpeted for everyone to hear. The classical front of the G.P.O., with its Ionic pillars and portico, was to serve as an admirable background for Pearse reading the proclamation, as it was to be an awe-inspiring sight on Friday night, its pillars and roof wrapped in tongues of flame, amid the swelling orchestration of rifle-fire, machine-gun chatter, bursting hand-grenades and booming artillery, presenting a Wagnerian grand finale to Easter Week.

Fortune can be capricious and thwart the bravest of men, but the very flourish with which Pearse and his companions began the rising drew down the favour of the god of war and set rapidly in motion a series of events which might seem unreal in a novel by Alexandre Dumas or the Baroness Orczy. The dramatic incidents were vivid not because they had the terrifying character of huge armies, impersonal, implacable, and bloody – as were at this time darkening the landscape in northern France and Belgium – but because they laid bare the heroic qualities of individual men and women afire with an all-consuming conviction. For once, and for a brief space, the god of war was marching with the small battalions.

One colourful incident after another builds up the dramatic quality and tension of the story – the vital messages passing from Dublin through New York to Berlin, most of them intercepted by the British intelligence service; the epic of the *Aud,* setting out from Germany, disguised as a cargo ship under the command of the resourceful Captain Karl Spindler, loaded with guns and ammunition for the rising, running the gauntlet of storm and British naval patrols, arriving unscathed near Tralee Bay on Holy Thursday afternoon; during those same days another German vessel, the submarine U-19, rapidly nosing its way by surface and under water, with the quixotic Sir Roger Casement aboard, to Tralee Bay; meantime the explosive confrontation between MacNeill and Pearse in Dublin as the truth of the conspiracy became known to MacNeill; the commands and countermands from Irish Volunteer headquarters; the midnight meetings and nightmare hours on Saturday and Sunday in Liberty Hall, Woodtown Park, and the Viceregal Lodge; the secret couriers hurrying throughout the country.

And then the rising itself so full of the bizarre – the Magazine Fort seized under cover of a well-kicked football; Cathal Brugha in the South Dublin Union, sitting propped up alone against a wall in a widening pool of blood from twenty-five wounds and blazing away at the British with his Peter the Painter as he sang 'God save Ireland'; the immortal thirteen at Mount Street Bridge, beating back the waves of raw British troops; the O'Rahilly, crumpled up in Sackville Lane, alone and mortally wounded, crying 'God help you, poor Ireland!', and tracing out a last note to his wife and children.

Love and harsh justice heightened the drama of the aftermath – Joseph Plunkett, already marked out for death by tuberculosis but condemned to execution by the British, marrying Grace Gifford by candlelight and with an armed guard as witnesses in Kilmainham Prison chapel four hours before he was shot; James Connolly, gravely wounded and unable to stand, strapped to a propped-up stretcher, as the target for a firing squad.

### James Stephens — the first literary voice

Here were all the tragic elements required by the ballad writer or, at a higher level, by the literary artist. Within a fortnight of the surrender Dublin was ringing with a come-all-ye ballad bewailing O'Rahilly's poignant death, but the ballad writers were not the first to rally to the defeated cause. The literary set, as quick to recognise idealism as they were to shrink from bloodshed, resented the attack on any of their fraternity and sprang to the defence while the rebellion was still in progress. James Stephens, the leprechaun-like character, sensing that here was a patriotic crock of gold he had overlooked, was early into print with his *Insurrection in Dublin*. This little book, which is in fact a diary written day by day during the rising and immediately afterwards, has all the impact of an eye-witness account by a skilled novelist. It was first published in 1916 and ran to a second impression that same year; a second edition was issued in 1919, and a third edition made a timely appearance in 1966.[8] The wonder is not that it has seen three editions but that it has not been reprinted more often. It is one of the memorable literary pieces of the rising.

What is remarkable about Stephens's little book is not its diamond-hard literary quality but its foreshadowing of the future. It was not just that he was already dismissing Redmond and the powerful Parliamentary Party, which the Irish people did not decisively do until the general election of December 1918, but that he showed both insight and fore-sight in his attitude to England, to Ulster, in his interpretation of the rising.

To England he made no concessions about its dismal record in Ireland:[9]

> We are a little country and you, a huge country, have persistently beaten us. We are a poor country and you, the richest country in the world, have persistently robbed us. That is the historical fact, and whatever national or political necessities are opposed in reply, it is true that you have never given Ireland any reason to love you, and you cannot claim her affection without hypocrisy or stupidity . . . No nation has forgiven its enemies as we have forgiven you, time after time down the miserable generations, the continuity of our forgive-ness only equalled by the continuity of your ill-treatment.

[8] Ed. Michael Adams, Dublin, Scepter Publishers, 1966.

[9] Ibid., p. 68.

After Stephens finished his book the executions of the rebel leaders took place. By the time he was writing the foreword to it on 8 May the message of Pearse's blood-sacrifice came home to him with startling clarity. He now wrote defiantly, 'If freedom is to come to Ireland − as I believe it is − then the Easter Insurrection was the only thing that could have happened'. Ireland, he argued, could not with any shred of self-respect, after centuries of sacrifice and heroism, meekly accept Home Rule as a gift grudgingly given:[10]

> The blood of brave men had to sanctify such a consummation if the national imagination was to be stirred to the dreadful business which is the organising of freedom; and both imagination and brains have been stagnant in Ireland this many a year.

Stephens's declaration is highly significant. Here is a literary man, Anglo-Irish by breed and background, middle-class and non-Catholic, making public profession of faith in the blood-sacrifice doctrine which was to become central in the credo of the extreme Irish republicans and which continues to animate young Irishmen and Irishwomen.

### Stephen MacKenna and *Memories of the Dead*

If Stephens was detached in his view of the rising, at least during Easter Week, it was otherwise with Stephen MacKenna.[11] This restless ailing writer shared with AE (George Russell) and Stephens the reputation of being the most fascinating conversationalist in Dublin literary circles. In 1916 he was slaving to complete the first of his five volumes, the translation of Plotinus, but all the time he was nagged by the regret that twenty years previously he had not striven, body and soul, to become a master writer of the Irish language. He counted among his personal friends Arthur Griffith, Thomas MacDonagh, Eamonn Ceannt and other nationalists, but the rising came on him with a shock of complete surprise. He felt almost cheated by what had happened.

As soon as he heard the news on Easter Monday he hurried down, ill as he was, to O'Connell Street in time to hear Pearse read the proclamation of the Republic to the disheartening circle of onlookers.[12] Later, at about five o'clock in the afternoon, Austin Clarke, then a student, also made his way to O'Connell Street and found MacKenna still there, leaning weakly against an electric tram standard, looking terribly ill, his face deathly pale. MacKenna could find no sentence to express his

[10] Ibid., p. 11.

[11] See memoir of MacKenna by E.R. Dodds in *Journal and Letters of Stephen MacKenna,* ed. E.R. Dodds, London, 1936, pp. 3-89.

[12] See statement by Austin Clarke, ibid., pp. 50-1.

intensity of emotion except to murmur brokenly 'At last!' Clarke was moved as much by what he called MacKenna's 'tormented exaltation' as he was by the solemnity of the moment. MacKenna was still there, staring in front of him, when Clarke finally left.

Later in the week, on Tuesday or Wednesday, MacKenna hobbled back to the G.P.O. with the aid of a stick and offered his services to the insurgents. The offer was refused, but MacKenna in another way helped to ensure the success of the rising more effectively than if he had been allowed to man the barricades. In 1917 a pamphlet, *Memories of the Dead*, by an otherwise unknown 'Martin Daly', was published in Dublin and was an immediate success. It was suspected even then that MacKenna was the author, and this appeared to be confirmed when after his death there was found among his papers a list of the 'cuts' made by the British military censor in the manuscript of Martin Daly's work.[13]

There was no subtlety about *Memories of the Dead*; it set out to praise nine of the men who suffered death at the hands of the British — Casement, Ceannt, Tom Clarke, MacBride, Sheehy Skeffington, Mac-Donagh, the O'Rahilly, Peader Macken and Pearse. They were a representative selection, both by reason of their different temperaments and backgrounds and by the manner of their deaths — O'Rahilly and Macken (the moneyed man and the tradesman, both fervent Catholics) died in the fighting; Sheehy Skeffington (the lovable rationalist and eccentric) was murdered; Casement (the British consul turned revolutionary) was hanged; the rest died under the rifles of the execution squads. MacKenna's praise of the dead was not without its reservations; he stated, for example, that though Pearse had a remarkable magnetism he had no particular charm of manner, and that for all O'Rahilly's enthusiasm for the Irish language he never mastered it. Yet the overall message of the pamphlet was plainly a salute of homage to the dead men and to their living ideals.

### The rally of the literary men

MacKenna was not typical of his literary fellows; he was a Gaelic Leaguer and a rebel born. But any reservations that other literary men, such as Stephens, had about the rising were cancelled out after the executions began. Padraic and Mary Colum, then in America, were first startled by the news of the rising, but once the executions had taken place they became advocates of the dead; Padraic Colum edited *Poems of the Irish Revolutionary Brotherhood* at Boston in the autumn of 1916. AE in Dublin wrote 'Salutation — written for those who took part in the 1916

[13] Ibid., p. 52.

Rebellion'; Francis Ledwidge, wearing the British uniform in which he was to die in the trenches in France, paid his tribute to Thomas Mac-Donagh:

> He shall not hear the bittern cry
> In the wild sky, where he is lain.

The American, Joyce Kilmer, who was to come to Europe with the American Expeditionary Force and like Ledwidge die in France as an ally of Great Britain, recalled what Yeats had written in September 1913 and chided him for it:

> 'Romantic Ireland's dead and gone
> It's with O'Leary in the grave'
> Then, Yeats, what gave that Easter dawn
> A hue so radiantly brave?

The rally of the bards to the 1916 standard had begun. Other writers and poets followed. They were fascinated as much by the gallant hopelessness of the rising as by its high-flung idealism. And undoubtedly there was a prickly *camaraderie,* that uneasy freemasonry, which binds together the artists, the poets, the writers. An unexpected ally in this camp was George Bernard Shaw, who once again exasperated his admiring British public by publishing a letter in the *Daily News* of 10 May 1916, protesting against the execution of the Irish leaders:

> My own view is that the men who were shot in cold blood, after their capture or surrender, were prisoners of war, and that it was, therefore, entirely incorrect to slaughter them ... I remain an Irishman, and am bound to contradict any implication that I can regard as a traitor any Irishman taken in a fight for Irish Independence against the British Government, which was a fair fight in everything except the enormous odds my countrymen had to face.

The following day John Dillon, who had witnessed the fighting at close quarters in Dublin and had every reason to condemn the rising as a mortal wound inflicted on the Irish Parliamentary Party to which he had devoted his life, stood up in the House of Commons to speak his mind on the executions he had striven so hard to prevent. His pent-up rage erupted like hot lava over the honourable members:[14]

> You are letting loose a river of blood, and make no mistake about it, between two races who, after three hundred years of hatred and strife, we had nearly succeeded in bringing together. Is that nothing? It is the fruit of our life-work. We have risked our lives a hundred

[14] Hansard, vol. 82, May 1916, p. 940.

times to bring about this result . . . and you are washing out our whole life-work in a sea of blood.

This was more than his listeners could bear but he disregarded their angry interruptions as he made his public act of national faith,

> I am not ashamed to say in the House of Commons that I am proud of these men . . . I say I am proud of their courage and if you were not so obtuse and stupid . . . you could have these men fighting for you . . . it is the insurgents who have fought a clean fight, a brave fight, however misguided, and it would have been a damned good thing for you if your soldiers were able to put up as good a fight as did these men in Dublin — 3,000 men against 20,000 with machine-guns and artillery.

## Yeats and the 'heroic, tragic lunacy'

These outspoken interventions by Shaw and Dillon were so unexpected that many wondered all the more why the Irish Oracle, Yeats, had not pronounced. At Easter 1916 he was staying with Sir William Rothenstein in Gloucestershire and was far from showing any initial flush of enthusiasm when he first heard about the rising. Rather did he cast a cold eye on it, and his first known impulse was to describe the rebel leaders as 'innocent and patriotic theorists, carried away by their belief that they must put their theories into practice. They would fail and pay the penalty for rashness.'[15] Even on 8 May, with the knowledge that already the Pearse brothers, Clarke, MacDonagh, Plunkett, Daly, O'Hanrahan and MacBride had been laid in quicklime in Dublin, he could write to Lady Gregory about the 'heroic, tragic lunacy of Sinn Fein'.[16] But a short visit to ravaged Dublin in early June roused the indomitable Irishry in him and this was strengthened by Maud Gonne MacBride when he stayed with her in Normandy that summer. The result was his 'Easter 1916' in which his complete conversion to admiration for the executed men was expressed in wonder, almost in awe, ending in the memorable refrain, 'A terrible beauty is born'. Later, in other poems, notably in his 'Rose Tree', 'Sixteen Dead Men', and 'The O'Rahilly' he re-affirmed his admiration for the men and their deed.

## The 'Faith and Fatherland' interpretation

The enthusiasm for the rising aroused among the poets and writers after

[15] Sir William Rothenstein in *Scattering Branches,* ed. Stephen Gwynn, London, 1940, pp. 46-7.

[16] Cited by Joseph Hone, *W.B. Yeats, 1865-1939,* London, 1942, p. 299. See the excellent article by Professor George Mayhew, 'A corrected typescript of Yeats's "Easter 1916"', in *The Huntington Library Quarterly,* 27, 1963, pp. 53-71. Also see E. Malins, *Yeats and the Easter Rising,* Dublin, Dolmen Press, 1965.

the execution of the leaders had much to do with the change of popular opinion towards the rebels. At a humbler but hardly less important level an influence was also exerted by newspaper men in Dublin, a number of whom had very definite separatist convictions. Piaras Beaslai, who worked in the *Freeman's Journal,* was second-in-command under Edward Daly at the Four Courts. Other newspaper men such as Fred Cogley of the *Irish Independent* and Sean Lester of the *Freeman's Journal* did not take part in the rising but were in sympathy with it. And J.J. O'Kelly ('Sceilg') as editor of the *Catholic Bulletin* used his magazine most effectively during 1916 and 1917 to propagate the notion that the rising was but the latest phase of the struggle for Faith and Fatherland. For the first time in centuries all the leaders of a rebellion were Catholics; full play was made of the undoubted mystical character of the writings of Pearse and Plunkett, the resolute religious practice of men like Ceannt and Mallin, and the striking fact that the rank and file of the Volunteers, almost to a man, prepared for the rising by going to confession and holy communion. MacKenna also, in *Memories of the Dead,* drew attention to the religious character of several of the leaders.

One of the Volunteers in the G.P.O., Brian O'Higgins, was constantly during the 1930s and 1940s to present this view of the rising through the pages of the *Wolfe Tone Annual* of which he was editor. It was a view he had already propounded in his booklet, *The Soldier's Story of Easter Week,* written in 1917 and first published in 1925. It was repeatedly reprinted and a special edition was issued in 1966 by one of O'Higgins's sons. He was a man of simple charm and deadly firm convictions; his account of Easter Week is told with full assurance that the angels were all on one side. In his own words:[17]

> The Rising of 1916 was a spiritual victory over selfishness, expedience and compromise and materialism, a victory for which Ireland should humbly and gratefully thank God through all the years of time.

This is Pearse speaking through the mouth of O'Higgins, and is evidence of how effective has been the interpretation of Irish history as propounded by Pearse in his writings, in his speeches (notably in his oration at the graveside of O'Donovan Rossa), and in the Proclamation of the Republic.

Though Brian O'Higgins is here selected because he was so faithful a disciple of the Pearse interpretation of Irish history and the most persistent propagator of the 'Faith and Fatherland' view of 1916, he has had many companions who have echoed the same or similar sentiments,

[17] *The Soldier's Story of Easter Week,* Dublin, 1966 ed., p. 93.

sometimes with the 'Fatherland' becoming also the religious faith. As might be expected a colourful crop of such publications appeared in 1966 to commemorate the Easter Rising. Five of these may be mentioned as representative; their very titles indicate how fully the Pearse interpretation has become part of the political folk tradition — *Deathless Glory* by Brendan Mary MacThormaid (the pen-name of a prominent ecclesiastic); *The Glorious Seven* by Seamus O'Kelly; *Sixteen Roads to Golgotha* by Martin Shannon; *Our Own Red Blood* by Sean Cronin; *Cry Blood, Cry Erin* by Redmond Fitzgerald.[18]

The academic historian may knowingly shake his head, confident that Pearse and his followers have misinterpreted Irish history, but in fact it has not been the academic historians, nor even the James Stephenses and the Stephen MacKennas but the Brian O'Higginses who have directly influenced the political views of Irish youth between 1916 and 1972. The Pearse-O'Higgins view of Irish history may be inaccurate (simply because it is one-sided) but it has sent and is sending young men out to die more certainly than did the *Cathleen ni Houlihan* of Yeats. The letters and diaries of Sean South and Fergal O'Hanlon, both of whom were killed during the I.R.A. foray against Brookeborough police barracks, Northern Ireland, on 1 January 1957, show them to have been dedicated idealists as fervent in their religious practice as they were in their republicanism.

### O'Casey, Behan and O'Flaherty

Case-hardened playwrights such as Brendan Behan and Sean O'Casey have poured scorn on the mentality bred, as a result of the rising, among the young Irish republicans after 1916. O'Casey in his *Shadow of a Gunman* lampoons the fanatical outlook of the young patriots:[19]

> I wish to God it was all over. The country is gone mad. Instead of counting their beads now they're countin' bullets; their Hail Marys and paternosters are burstin' bombs — burstin' bombs, an' the rattle of machine-guns; petrol is their holy water; their Mass is a burnin' buildin'; their *De Profundis* is *The Soldiers' Song*, an' their creed is, I believe in the gun almighty, maker of heaven an' earth — an' it's all for 'the glory o' God an' the honour o' Ireland'.

Behan in *The Hostage* jibes at the high moral code and ruthless

[18] Brendan Mary MacThormaid, *Deathless Glory*, Dublin, 1966; Seamus G. O'Kelly, *The Glorious Seven, 1916-1966*, 2nd ed., Dublin, Irish News Service and Publicity, 1966; Martin Shannon, *Sixteen Roads to Golgotha*, Dublin, Red Hand Books, 1966; Sean Cronin, *Our Own Red Blood*, Dublin, Wolfe Tone Society, 1966; Redmond Fitzgerald, *Cry Blood, Cry Erin*, London, 1966.

[19] *The Shadow of a Gunman*, in Sean O'Casey, *Collected Plays*, 1, London, 1953, p. 131.

political principles of the I.R.A. captors of Leslie, the British Tommy, and pillories their young leader who has modelled himself so faithfully on the principles of Pearse. Yet neither O'Casey nor Behan could shake off fully the reverence they had learned for 'the pure true Irish republican' in their younger days; O'Casey shows it for example in *The Plough and the Stars,* in the persons of Lieutenant Langon of the Irish Volunteers and Captain Brennan of the Citizen Army, as does Behan for the I.R.A. officer in *The Hostage,* despite the barbed shafts at I.R.A. ideals. Liam O'Flaherty's *The Informer* is a powerful work but its revolutionary leader, Commandant Dan Gallagher, is set in a seamy background which bears little or no relation to I.R.A. activity during the War of Independence.

O'Flaherty in *The Informer,* published in 1925, showed his sharp, almost bitter appreciation of republican ideals during the War of Independence. By the time his *Insurrection* appeared in 1950 he is expressing himself with frank admiration for the ideals of the 1916 leaders. The book is confined to a vivid account of events in Dublin during Easter Week, when the central character, Bartly Madden, a wild Connemara boy newly returned from munition work in England, is caught up by accident in the rebellion. O'Flaherty's realism struggles with his reverence for Pearse and the insurgent leaders. The story is resolved when Madden, refusing to surrender with the leaders, goes out alone with a pistol in each hand to shoot it out with the British soldiers.

When all has been said, when the hilarious sarcasm of O'Casey, the bawdy wit of Behan, and the distorted realism of O'Flaherty have had their opportunities to colour the popular outlook in 1916, it remains true that it is Pearse's own interpretation which has persisted.

The outlook of the young I.R.A. man has been neatly summed up by Timothy P. Coogan in his *Ireland since the Rising:*[20]

His is a world of midnight tramping on lonely hillsides, of secret drilling, of absolute loyalty and immaculate purity. Apart from the occasional thug who inevitably crops up in such a movement, the typical I.R.A. man is a quiet affable character who leads a life of Carthusian virtue both in speech and private conduct, and with a scrupulous dedication to religious observance from which all the Church's denunciations of his organisation cannot budge him. Ireland's history — its grimmer parts — are as familiar to him as his own name; Ireland's Gaelic culture is his inspiration. Republicanism and the Irish language are the two issues on which a young Irishman will

[20] *Ireland Since the Rising,* London, 1966, p. 268. How accurately Coogan expresses the mentality of the I.R.A. may be seen from the memoir of an ex-I.R.A. member, Sean O'Callaghan, *The Easter Lily,* 2nd ed., London, 1967.

defy and upbraid a bishop. Arguments against taking human life will not move him.

### The voices of the executed leaders

The executions, the widespread arrests and then the release of prisoners in 1917, above all the threat of conscription in 1918, increased tenfold the significance of the 1916 message. The literary men had led the rally and this was reinforced by the voices of the executed leaders when their works were published and re-published. MacDonagh's *Literature in Ireland* was with the printers at the time of the rising and was published shortly afterwards, in June. Plunkett's poems were edited that same year by his sister, Geraldine. Colum edited, at Boston in 1916, a selection of poetry by the dead leaders.

Nowhere was the 1916 message clearer than in Pearse's writings and it was these which received the greatest welcome. Pearse, in making his personal arrangements for the rising, had appointed as his literary executor a former pupil of his, Desmond Ryan, who was then a university student staying at St Enda's. Ryan fought under Pearse in the G.P.O., was imprisoned in England, and after his release in July 1917 set about fulfilling the task to which he had been appointed by Pearse. He found an eager audience and many helpers, among whom perhaps the most influential was a brilliant young Maynooth professor, Dr Patrick Browne.

Before the rising Fr Browne had been associated in the Gaelic League and cultural movement with Pearse and the separatists. The night before Sean MacDermott was executed Fr Browne was with him in Kilmainham Jail. It was not surprising, therefore, that Fr Browne was asked to write the introduction to a volume of Pearse's collected works. Even Pearse would have been satisfied with Browne's comments, which concluded:[21]

> His name and deeds will be taught by mothers to their children long before the time when they will be learned in school histories. To older people he will be a watchword in the national fight, a symbol of the unbroken continuity and permanence of the Gaelic tradition. And they will think of him forever in different ways, as a soldier who died for it, as a martyr who bore witness with his blood to the truth of his faith, as a hero, a second Cuchulainn, who battled with a divine frenzy to stem the waves of the invading tide.

Elsewhere in the introduction Browne fuses together religion and nationality into that alluring concept of 'Faith and Fatherland' which was to be expounded so constantly and so successfully by men like Brian O'Higgins during the succeeding decades.

[21] *Collected works of Padraic H. Pearse: plays, stories, poems,* Dublin, 1917, p. xix. Fr Browne's introduction is dated from Maynooth, 21 May 1917.

Appropriately it was Desmond Ryan who published in 1919 *The Man Called Pearse,* the first biography of his beloved headmaster. Ryan's attitude to Pearse at this time is best summed up by the entry in his diary on re-visiting St Enda's after release from prison:[22]

> Dream sensation still endures. Might be a rush of boys in any minute. Pearse's study very silent. Pausing in his bedroom I stooped and kissed his pillow.

The biography is a small work, more an impression and recollections than a full-length study, but is nevertheless quite effective.

## The rising established, 1966

By 1966, at the time of the golden jubilee celebrations of the rising, the success of the men of Easter Week was complete, at least externally, in the Republic of Ireland. Church and State, Catholic, Protestant and Jew, local and national bodies of all kinds vied with one another to do homage to the rebels of fifty years before. This is fully demonstrated in the illustrated publication, *Cuimhneachán, 1916-1966: a record of Ireland's commemoration of the 1916 rising,* produced by the Department of External Affairs, Dublin. The change in public opinion over fifty years was significant in a number of instances. On Easter Monday Cardinal Conway presided at High Mass in St Patrick's Cathedral, Armagh, to mark the jubilee. His predecessor at the time of the rising, Cardinal Logue, had denounced the rising as a 'lamentable disturbance', as had the Protestant primate in even stronger language; the *Irish Independent* and *Irish Times,* both of which had called down dire punishment on the captured rebel leaders in 1916, produced excellent illustrated supplements to commemorate the event; Trinity College, Dublin, had been the military centre from which the rebellion had been crushed, but in 1966 the provost of Trinity College, Dr McConnell, had a framed copy of the proclamation of the republic hanging in his study; most piquant of all was the special illustrated supplement section devoted to the 1916 rising by the *Irish Tatler and Sketch.* The ghosts of the British officers who attended Fairyhouse Races on Easter Monday would goggle in disbelief to see in this social magazine of their class the message, truculently expressed, which had been read out on that day in more lofty phrases at the G.P.O.:[23]

Generation after generation had taken up arms in desperation against

[22] D. Ryan, *Remembering Sion,* London, 1934, p. 217.

[23] Liam Robinson, 'The Road to Freedom', in *Irish Tatler and Sketch: Ireland's premier social and sporting monthly,* April 1966, p. 23.

misrule and for the ideal of self-determination. Never for long were the conquerors allowed to settle smugly in their pernicious state of absenteeism and belief that the odd bone tossed to the Celt would keep him quiet.

Another saga has been added to the heroic cycle of Irish history, but historians will look askance at what to them is at best a glamorised, and at worst a prejudiced, version of the facts.

## MacNeill and the inner story

The first sharp question mark against the accepted story about 1916 appeared in March 1961 with the publication in *Irish Historical Studies* of two memoranda by Eoin MacNeill.[24] Rarely if ever in Ireland has the appearance of a historical record received such immediate attention at a popular level. Two of the principal national daily newspapers, the *Irish Press* and the *Irish Independent,* displayed posters announcing the publication of the documents, and it was included as an item in the 1 p.m. news bulletin from Radio Eireann on the day of publication. The national daily and evening newspapers ran a series of articles analysing and commenting on the memoranda. The reason for the welcome reception was satisfaction at discovering the true story of MacNeill's behaviour during those hectic days and nights just before Easter Week. Even extreme republicans after Easter Week had not doubted his integrity but they regarded his conduct as inexplicable, due either to personal weakness or to that legendary professorial lack of reality. But even a university professor was expected to act logically and consistently, and on the face of it MacNeill had done neither on the eve of Easter Week, even though his record over twenty years in the Gaelic League and the Volunteers had shown him to be both logical and consistent.

In the memoranda two shocks were administered, the first to the Pearse interpretation of Easter Week, the second to the Pearse image. The significance of the first memorandum was that it was written by MacNeill as chief-of-staff of the Irish Volunteers, in mid-February 1916, over two months before the rising, and therefore could not be considered as a piece of self-exculpation composed in order to justify his policy and behaviour during those momentous four days immediately before the rising. It was written for the benefit of Pearse, Plunkett, Ceannt and MacDonagh, the four members of the Irish Volunteer Headquarters Staff who favoured an insurrection whether or not the British moved

[24] Edited by F.X. Martin in *Irish Historical Studies,* XII, no. 47, March 1961, pp. 226-71. It is the only time that an issue of *I.H.S.* has been exhausted at the time of publication and required a reprint to meet popular demand.

against the Volunteers. In the memorandum MacNeill considered the blood-sacrifice proposal and dismissed it as irrelevant to the circumstances prevailing in Ireland at that time.

In dealing with the various arguments advanced to justify an armed revolt MacNeill showed a pragmatic power of judgment which belies the impression of him, later circulated by advocates of the rising, that he was of a purely speculative and scholarly mind. As a professor of history he made short work of the argument that 'Ireland has always struck too late'.

On the question of a rising his own view was crisply summed up in the declaration:[25]

> To my mind, those who feel impelled towards military action on any of the grounds that I have stated are really impelled by a sense of feebleness or despondency or fatalism or by an instinct of satisfying their own emotions or escaping from a difficult and complex and trying situation. It is our duty, if necessary, to trample on our personal feelings and to face every sort of difficulty and complexity, and to think only of our country's good.

The second memorandum, written some time between June and October 1917, gives MacNeill's account of the events leading up to the outbreak of the rising, especially what happened between Spy Wednesday and Easter Monday. It emerges clearly that MacNeill had been deceived in particular by Pearse, MacDermott, Plunkett and MacDonagh, and that at least Pearse and Plunkett had lied to him about their intentions. It makes sorry reading, but also makes intelligible what had hitherto appeared so confusing about the orders and countermanding orders to the Volunteers during Holy Week. It explains why MacDonagh left behind him a letter to clear MacNeill's reputation, and why Pearse and MacDermott who were well aware of the intrigues which had deluded MacNeill took care before their executions to exonerate him of any charge of treachery or broken faith. The striking fact is that MacNeill, with that imperturbability which was one of his characteristics, did not seek during his lifetime to publish the memoranda or to justify his conduct at the time of the rising. Perhaps as a historian he fondly believed that sooner or later historians catch up on the truth.

Can the rising be justified morally?
It is no easy task to justify the rising on democratic or theological principles. There is no doubt that the rebellion had no popular support;

[25] In *I.H.S.*, loc. cit., p. 236.

this is one fact on which the British authorities and the Irish insurgents agreed.

The traditional theological conditions required for lawful revolt seem at first sight, and even at second, to be absent in 1916. Firstly, the government must be a tyranny, that is, ruling by force against the will of the governed. There are four further conditions — the impossibility of removing the tyranny except by bloodshed, that the evil of the tyranny be greater than the ill-effects of the revolt, serious probability of success, and finally the approval of the community as a whole.

Few revolts would have been undertaken if the rebels had waited to ensure that they satisfied the requirements of the theologians. Pearse, Clarke, Connolly and their followers argued from other than the traditional theological principles. They regarded themselves as what Jacques Maritain calls 'the prophetic shock-minority' whose duty was to rouse the people from a hypnotic slumber. And, Maritain comments, 'People as a rule prefer to sleep. Awakenings are always bitter.'[26] The rebel leaders believed that Ireland was on the point of losing its national identity, its soul, and that bloodshed was a lesser evil. Pearse faced the problem squarely (even if inadequately, according to strict theological reasoning) when he declared:[27]

> Bloodshed is a cleansing and sanctifying thing and the nation which regards it as the final horror has lost its manhood. There are many things more horrible than bloodshed; and slavery is one of them.

For many of the present generation this is a disturbing declaration, but it was expressed in similar phrases, amid the applause of the Free World, by Churchill during Great Britain's desperate struggle with Nazi Germany in World War II.[28] Pearse began to see a sacred character in the grim visage of war; in December 1915 he confidently informed his readers:[29]

> War is a terrible thing, but war is not an evil thing . . . Many people in Ireland dread war because they do not know it. Ireland has not known the exhilaration of war for over a hundred years.

And Pearse used more frightening expressions. Looking at the ravaged blood-stained soil of France and Flanders, and the daily carnage of

[26] J. Maritain, *Man and the State*, ed. R. O'Sullivan, London, 1954, p. 129.

[27] P.H. Pearse, *Political Writings and Speeches*, Dublin, 1917, p. 99.

[28] See, e.g., W. Churchill, *The Unrelenting Struggle: War-speeches 1940-41*, ed. C. Eade, London, 1942.

[29] Pearse, *Political Writings*, p. 217.

thousands of soldiers on the Western and Eastern fronts, he exclaimed:[30]

> The last sixteen months have been the most glorious in the history
> of Europe. Heroism has come back to the earth . . . It is good for the
> world that such things should be done. The old heart of the earth
> needed to be warmed with the red wine of the battlefield. Such
> august homage was never before offered to God as this, the homage
> of millions of lives given gladly for the love of country.

This purple passage caused James Connolly to explode in exaspera-
tion, 'No! We do not think that the old heart of the earth needs to be
warmed with the red wine of millions of lives. We think anyone who
does is a blithering idiot!'[31] Connolly was the realist, seeing the unfortunate soldiers in the trenches not as so many symbols of nationality
but as suffering individuals.

### The blood-sacrifice ideal

The doctrine which Pearse was propounding, the blood-sacrifice ideal,
was not peculiar to his own cast of mind though he may have expressed
it in more startling terms than did his fellow-rebels.[32] Joseph Plunkett
and Terence MacSwiney in their poetry, Sean MacDermott and Thomas
MacDonagh in their speeches, were at one with Pearse in this notion.[33]
One far-seeing patriot, a friend of all these men, raised his shrill voice in
warning. Francis Sheehy Skeffington, the pacifist, published an open
letter to MacDonagh in May 1915.[34] MacDonagh had taken the opportunity at a Women's Protest Meeting to extol the virtues of armed force,
and boasted of being one of the creators of a new militarism in Ireland.
Skeffington warned him that this might well lead to 'crimson the fields
of Ireland. For us that would be disaster enough', and ended with the
exhortation that MacDonagh should 'think it over, before the militarist
current draws you too far from your humanitarian anchorage'. Ironically,
Skeffington was to be executed by the British during the rising in which
MacDonagh took a leading part.

[30] Ibid., p. 216.

[31] In T.P. Coogan, *Ireland since the Rising*, p. 11.

[32] For Pearse's doctrine of the 'blood-sacrifice' see Pearse, *Political Writings*,
pp. 87, 91-9, 215-18, and in particular his play 'The Singer' and his poem 'The Fool'.
The subject demands a special study.

[33] See notes by F.X. Martin in *I.H.S.*, XII, no. 47, March 1961, p. 241.

[34] F. Sheehy Skeffington, 'An open letter to Thomas MacDonagh', in *The
Irish Citizen*, 22 May 1915, reprinted separately in 1915, and again reprinted in
*Irish Times*, 12 March 1966, p. 10.

Although Connolly had reacted indignantly against Pearse's 'red wine of the battlefield' declaration he himself had, at the time of the O'Donovan Rossa funeral in August 1915, written of the need for the members of the Irish Citizen Army to be willing to lay down their lives to keep alive the soul of the nation.[35] By 5 February 1916 he had progressed so far in agreement with the blood-sacrifice ideal that he could write:[36]

> Without the slightest trace of irreverence but in all due humility and awe, we recognise that of us, as of mankind before Calvary, it may truly be said 'without the shedding of Blood there is no Redemption'

The scriptural imagery which Connolly was using had long been part of the texture of Pearse's thought. He saw himself in the role of the scapegoat, the man of sorrows on whom the political salvation of Ireland would depend. 'One man', he wrote, 'can free a people as one Man redeemed the world'.

## The cult of bloodshed

British political and military events during the three years before the rising largely explain how the explosive situation was allowed to develop in Ireland. It was not only that Great Britain, inextricably entangled in European affairs, allowed Irish separatists more rope than she would normally permit, but the appalling character of the war made bloodshed a commonplace and carnage an accepted fact. At the second battle of Artois in May-June 1915 the French under Pétain advanced a mere three miles with a loss of 400,000 men. The British at Gallipoli, with strong Irish contingents, were savagely repulsed by the Turks. Worse was to come at the battle of the Somme, in 1916, where the British lost 400,000 and the French 200,000; the German losses rose to near 500,000. The climax of horror was when the British found they had 60,000 casualties after one incredible day of German shell, bullet and gas.

In Ireland, as all over Europe, war was being extolled by the recruiting sergeants, by the newspapers, by the leaders of society. The poets, Rupert Brooke in England and Charles Péguy in France, were singing exultantly of war and the shedding of blood for the patriot cause. Little wonder then that Pearse could exclaim that 'bloodshed is a cleansing and sanctifying thing'. Even Eoin MacNeill accepted the validity of the blood-sacrifice ideal, but in a memorandum of February 1916 he denied

[35] J. Connolly, 'Why the Citizen Army honours Rossa', in *Diarmuid Ó Donnabhain Rosa, 1831-1915: Souvenir*, Dublin, 1915, pp. 18-19.

[36] In *The Workers' Republic*, 5 February 1916.

that it applied to the circumstances of Ireland at that time.[37]

But once Pearse and his companions decided that they had the right to organise a revolt their feet were on a slope, slippery with more than blood. A rebellion meant a conspiracy, and a conspiracy meant deception, deception not only of their enemies, the British, but of their colleagues, MacNeill, O'Rahilly, Hobson, O'Connell, Fitzgibbon and others. It became necessary to lie and deceive. None of this would lie heavily on the gay shoulders of Sean MacDermott who would dismiss it, almost laughingly, as part of 'the ruse of war', but for a man such as Pearse with a strict code it was painful to pursue a policy of deceiving his colleagues. The rising was to come as a relief from all the double-talk in which he had been involved for months on end.

### Imagination and insurrection

The fantasy, the imagination of the rebel leaders, was an expression of the artistic mind in the realm of politics. One of the most important books on the rising, William Irwin Thompson's *The Imagination of an Insurrection: Dublin, Easter 1916,* was published in New York by the Oxford University Press in 1967. Thompson's conclusions come remarkably close to the view expounded in this survey, namely that the rising was a drama conceived on an imaginative, not on a military level.

When Birrell was being questioned on 19 May 1916 by the royal commission on the causes of the rebellion he gave special attention to the Irish literary renaissance and asserted that its many products were[38]

all characterised by originality and independence of thought and expression, quite divorced from any political party, and all tending towards, and feeding latent desires for, some kind of separate Irish National existence. It was a curious situation to watch, but there was nothing in it suggestive of revolt or rebellion except in the realm of thought.

Thompson, without adverting to Birrell's assertion, traces the process by which Ireland passed from thought to action, from a literary revolt to an armed rebellion. Rightly he dwells on Standish James O'Grady whose popular histories of pre-Christian Ireland, published during the last quarter of the nineteenth century, recreated a world of heroes and heroines. But, as Thompson observes (p.22), O'Grady's history is 'not simply a retelling of past events but a conjuration that overwhelms the present, and, further, gives the present its full meaning'. A new and

[37] In memorandum of February 1916 edited in *I.H.S.*, XII, no. 47, March 1961, p. 236.

[38] In *Royal Commission on the Rebellion in Ireland,* London, 1916, p. 21(a).

exciting cycle of Irish history is presented with Cú Chulainn as its great hero. O'Grady's concept is an Irish version of Wagner's *Ring*.

Thompson points out that O'Grady was politically irrelevant in 1878, his own day, but not in 1916. It was reading O'Grady and Sir Samuel Ferguson that caused Yeats to turn to the heroic period of Irish history. In 1889 he published *The Wanderings of Oisin,* and with it began the Irish Literary Renaissance. It was significant that it was the Fenian veteran, John O'Leary, who gathered enough subscriptions to convince the publishers to print it. From Yeats the line runs straight to Pearse with his glorification of Cú Chulainn, who became, as Desmond Ryan recalls, an invisible member of the staff at St Enda's College.

It is difficult, Thompson remarks (p.114), to tell where the artistic messianism of O'Grady and Yeats leaves off and the political messianism of Pearse begins. It was the encounter between literature and revolution. One night in 1899 O'Grady made a prophecy:[39] 'We have now a literary movement, it is not very important; it will be followed by a political movement, that will not be very important; then must come a military movement, that will be important indeed'. Pearse became head of the military movement which fulfilled O'Grady's prophecy. The rising came as a surprise to Yeats, but it won his admiration; in it he saw Pearse as the new Hero. It was fitting on that score that the monument unveiled in the G.P.O. to commemorate the rising should be Oliver Sheppard's bronze statue of Cú Chulainn.

Yet the Cú Chulainn statue is not an adequate representation of the spirit of the men of 1916 nor of Pearse's thought. Thompson points out (pp. 118-24) that though Pearse found in Cú Chulainn a stimulus he turned to Jesus Christ for a model — 'Pearse saw the role of the rebel as the perfect Imitation of Christ'. Suffering and death, redemption and resurrection; these were the stages Pearse saw as inevitable if Ireland were to recover her national soul which she was pathetically bartering for a mess of British colonial pottage.

Speaking at the Robert Emmet commemorative meeting at the Rotunda in March 1911 Pearse had declared that 'Dublin will have to do some great act to atone for the shame of not producing a man to dash his head against a stone wall in an effort to rescue Robert Emmet'. Here already were the notes of guilt, of a brave foolish deed, and of atonement, and by 1916 they were being expressed through the imagery of the passion and death of Christ. Pearse was willing to attempt that deed

---

[39] In Thompson, *The Imagination of an Insurrection: Dublin, Easter, 1916,* New York, 1967, p. 62.

alone, as he exclaimed in *The Singer*, 'One man can free a people as one Man redeemed the world. I will take no pike. I will go into the battle with bare hands.'

Thompson's book is an exceptional study, especially his analysis of Pearse (pp. 74-124), whom he presents cast and all. He does justice not only to Pearse and his fellow-rebels but to MacNeill and his group in the Irish Volunteers (p. 95): 'MacNeill had a perfect psychological understanding of the revolutionaries, so perfect, in fact, that their main excuse for concealing their plans from him was that they found him a hard man to approach'. The analysis of Pearse is only one part of the survey in which major attention is given to Yeats, AE, and Sean O'Casey. Thompson should be read by all who want to understand the Easter Rising.

### The hero and the fool

The rising caused many deaths and casualties; most of them were of innocent people. But one person to whom it dealt a mortal blow, who died unwept, unhallowed and unsung, was the stage Irishman. The Hero supplanted the Fool. Paddy the Irishman, complete with ragged clothes, crumpled hat, shillelagh, clay pipe, a snub nose and a mouthful of 'Begobs!' and 'Begorras!' disappeared from *Punch* and from view. Paddy no longer had a pig in the parlour; instead of a pig he had a Howth rifle or a stick of gelignite.

The Irish who had been the 'niggers' of the nineteenth-century Great Britain now emerged, in the words of Maud Gonne, with 'a tragic dignity'. Pearse had expressed it with intense feeling in *The Rebel:*

And because I am of the people, I understand the people . . .
Their shame is my shame, and I have reddened for it,
Reddened for that they have served, they who should be free,
Reddened for that they have gone in want, while others have been full,
Reddened for that they have walked in fear of lawyers and of their
   jailers
With their writs of summons and their handcuffs,
Men mean and cruel!

And he had gone on in a white-heat of feeling to prophesy and to warn:

And I say to my people's masters: Beware,
Beware of the thing that is coming, beware of the risen people,
Who will take what ye would not give.
Did ye think to conquer the people?
Or that Law is stronger than life and than men's desire to be free?
We will try it out with you, ye that have harried and held,
Ye that have bullied and bribed, tyrants, hypocrites, liars!

The servile and feckless peasant threw off his rags to reveal himself a disciplined, courageous soldier. In English eyes, the Irish were never the same again.

**5**

# Nationalism in Asia

## *Wang Gungwu*

Nationalism, as the preceding lectures in this series have once more indicated, is a vast subject. Its vastness, its complexity and its many elusive qualities have inspired continued effort to pin down its common features so that we may better understand nationalism as a concept and as a phenomenon. But so uncertain are we about its different manifestations, its roots, its primitive and modern forms and its widespread appeal that we are not always sure whether we are talking about something universal, very old and indestructible or about something relatively recent that has spread from Western Europe to all parts of the world. I shall therefore follow my predecessors in this series by limiting my use of the term nationalism. I shall confine myself to the historical phenomenon that first appeared in Asia a little over a hundred years ago as a reaction to Western power and dominance.

This is not to suggest that there was no idea of nation or national consciousness in Asia prior to the period of Western dominance. Beneath the universal religions of Buddhism and Islam and the cultural and social structures supported by Hinduism and Confucianism, there survived ancient concepts of kinship and tribe like the Sanskrit *vamsa* and the Chinese *tsu* which had been developed to cover the sense of identity of groups which behaved as nations did in Europe before the eighteenth century. Some of these peoples had also achieved national consciousness before modern times, most notably the Koreans sandwiched between the Chinese and the Japanese, the Vietnamese in their attitudes towards China, and the Burmans and the Thais in their attitudes towards each other. We can also include the Japanese in their attitudes towards Korea and China, the Chinese during the Sung and Ming dynasties in their attitudes towards the Mongols and various Manchurian military federations, and, less convincingly, various peoples living on the periphery of the Indian heartland, like the Bengalis, the Tamils and the Singhalese.

In these examples, the idea of nation was related to differences in language and aspects of culture as well as dynastic interests and some idea of territorial rights. Although one may question how strongly felt was this sense of nation, there is little doubt that many of the national differences perceived may be compared with those between nations in Europe at a similar stage of history. What is important to emphasise is that, at this stage, the only important differences were those between neighbours, either neighbours of roughly equal strength or small countries on the borders of large empires. The only exception was the Muslim threat to Hinduism and Buddhism which had a much wider significance, but the records suggest that this threat was still perceived principally as the physical threat of Islamised forces against neighbouring Hindu and Buddhist states in most of South and South-East Asia. The defence against physical threats from nearby powers encouraged the growth of national consciousness, but there was nothing in this period before the nineteenth century which resembled the reaction to Western dominance soon afterwards.

What of the reaction to Western advances into Asia during the sixteenth, seventeenth and eighteenth centuries? There were numerous battles between Asian armies and navies against sea-borne European forces, especially in South and South-East Asia. There were as many battles in North and Central Asia between Tsarist Russian troops and various Turks, Mongols, Manchus and Chinese. There were several local wars between Asian armies in which European soldiers and sailors fought for one side or the other. In addition, most of the Europeans fought one another as separate nations of Portuguese, Spaniards, Dutch, British and French, and often more bitterly among themselves than when they fought Asian armies. None of the European nations was dominant over any large area. They controlled a few ports and the major trade routes and the number of Asians ruled over by Europeans was very small. On the contrary, the Europeans seemed content to deal with Asian rulers and elites on equal terms and sought Asian allies against rival Europeans. In this way the profits of an expanding trade were shared by Europeans and Asians alike. Where there were discrepancies, there were conflicts, but these were conflicts between neighbouring nations, contiguous armies and rival ports. They were the normal battles between aggressors and defenders whose strengths were comparable and where each side expected sometimes to win and sometimes to lose. Nowhere was there overwhelming superiority. The Europeans had become accepted as local forces with strange faces whose strong home bases were too far away to arouse any widespread fears. They were no great danger to the larger Asian polities. On the contrary, the rulers of the smaller weak nations were often grateful for the protection and help some Europeans could give them against their Asian neighbours.

The picture began to change with the rise of Britain as a new kind of power and representing a new kind of civilisation. British dominance in India became totally unchallengeable by the turn of the nineteenth century. During the first half of that century, the British could have become dominant over the whole of South-East Asia if they had wanted to. They certainly became the dominant power along the coast of China by the middle of the century. Their threat to Dutch influence stimulated the Dutch to extend their power over most of Island South-East Asia. The French then joined in establishing themselves in Indo-China and in following the British up the China coast; and the Russians speeded up their advance across Northern and Central Asia. They were followed by the Americans and the Germans and this ended in the global scramble for what was left after the British and the French had taken what they wanted. But well before the end of the nineteenth century, it was obvious to Asian rulers and elites from India to Japan that the Western powers were in control. It was time to react against that dominance.

When it was that the reaction began, what forms it took and how successful each type of reaction was are subjects of controversy. One can approach the rise of nationalism in Asia in several ways. Nationalism did not appear immediately in any country, nor did all peoples turn to nationalism in defence against the West. Chronologically, Japan reacted sooner than China and, among colonial countries, India developed nationalism earlier than Indonesia and both were much earlier than, say, Cambodia and Malaya. In terms of size, the large entities like China, Japan and India initiated nationalist movements sooner than the smaller weaker countries. Also, more cohesive nations like Japan adopted nationalism easily while those less integrated territories met with greater difficulty in making their nationalism credible. Also, if we distinguish countries which were never colonised from those which came under actual Western rule, there are further differences: on the one hand, between Japan and China which sooner or later produced nationalism, and Thailand and Nepal which never found it necessary; and, on the other hand, between India, Indonesia, Burma and Vietnam whose nationalism became increasingly radical before independence, and Ceylon, Cambodia, Malaysia and Singapore whose nationalism seems more significant after independence than before. Finally, one cannot ignore the by-product nationalism of minority groups in the new nations, notably in the larger polities, of the Mongols and the Tibetans in China and of the Muslims in India who broke away to form Pakistan, and also of those who remained in India; and, in smaller nations, of the Karens in Burma, the Malays in Thailand, the Tamils in Ceylon and the Muslims in the Philippines, and, rather as a special problem by itself, of the Chinese minorities all over South-East Asia.

In short, if we take nationalism in Asia in all its possible forms, it is apt to become a very large bag into which are thrown a great variety of miscellaneous ideas, claims and fears. The various forms of nationalism may have features in common and may even be related to one another, but taken together as a mixed bag they are unlikely to have great significance for the understanding of the phenomenon of nationalism in modern history. I propose therefore to limit myself to the main thrust of nationalism in Asia which started in the late nineteenth and early twentieth centuries and examine the consequences of that nationalism today. I shall refer to variants of this nationalism from time to time, but only to illustrate special points of interest.

I have earlier pointed to the rise of British power in Asia as marking the beginning of change. What was important was not that the power was British, or that the British were unusually aggressive or exceptionally humanitarian. There was, in fact, no nationalistic response to the extensions of the British Empire. The important development was that the British advances opened up a new era of Western rivalry and that this new rivalry rose high above the political, economic and technological capacities of even the strongest Asian countries. No longer were Asian rulers and elites participants in that rivalry; no Western powers depended on them as allies or feared them as enemies as before. The Western powers were, for the first time, fighting their Western struggles in Asia above the heads of the Asians themselves. The various Asians had become almost irrelevant except as part of the domains of a particular power or as bargaining pieces. This was specially true of South and South-East Asia where even countries which did not become colonies, like Nepal and Thailand, were sovereign only by the goodwill or the agreement of Western powers. Only in East Asia had the Western powers been hesitant, and even there, the Chinese government by the end of the nineteenth century was rapidly becoming irrelevant in the decisions of Western powers. The fate of China alerted the Japanese and Japan alone reacted quickly enough to ward off the fate of the rest of Asia. It did so because it was the first Asian country to perceive that Asia was not simply being threatened by powerful aliens but by a new world order. It realised that there had been a qualitative change in Western rivalry over Asia, not as before competing to share what the Asians were prepared to offer but manoeuvring to share Asia itself among themselves.

In short, the British led the way to total Western supremacy in Asia. It was a supremacy assured by a new kind of civilisation built upon the Industrial Revolution, the liberation of bourgeois economic values and the cohesive nation-state. The supremacy was so overwhelming that the various Western powers settled their territories and interests between themselves, as with the Anglo-Dutch Treaty in 1824 settling their borders along the Straits of Malacca and the Anglo-French agreements to preserve the independence of Thailand. Where they could not agree to divide territory as in East Asia, they supported each other in forcing treaties upon the surviving Asian nations and, where there was enough to go around, they did their utmost to avoid open conflict among themselves.

The first reaction to the Western impact by both China and Japan recognised the physical supremacy of bigger guns and superior ships. But the Japanese went further and introduced large-scale political and economic reforms and even encouraged the entry of Western educational and cultural institutions. They prepared themselves to acquire the kind of power which made Western civilisation superior, and sought to reproduce the Industrial Revolution, the new economic values and a nationalistic state more or less simultaneously. The young Meiji leaders found that nationalism could be used as an instrument of centralisation against rival elite groups. Also, they succeeded in welding this nationalism on to their sense of Japan as destined to dominate parts of the Asian mainland, especially Korea. Not least, while they wished to establish a modern Western-type empire and become equal with the West, the nationalism was there to ensure that this empire could fit into a framework which still expressed the Japanese national essence.

The Japanese defeat of China in 1894-5 showed conclusively that mere technological borrowing was not enough and spurred the Chinese on to begin their series of political, economic and educational reforms. But these came too late to save the dynasty, or even the Confucian system of government. As a result, the Chinese were forced to reconstruct a new national polity to replace the dying one and this has taken them most of this century to achieve. Significantly, they found nationalism necessary to mobilise the people to save China, to stimulate the creative energies of new classes in order to master the new industrial civilisation. But the Chinese version, coming after a long series of humiliations, had less of the 'blood and iron' quality of Japanese nationalism. Instead it was a nationalism rooted in fear of enslavement, of dismemberment of the country, and of being at the lower end of a Social Darwinist table. The Chinese, as spoken for by Sun Yat-sen and Liang Ch'i-ch'ao, were afraid of going the way of India and the Ottoman Empire. They resented being treated as inferiors by Westerners; worse still, they resented having to admit that their civilisation could be inferior to that of the West. And, not least, they resented being treated as inferior to the Japanese. As a consequence, their nationalism was more infused with a mixture of despair and strident bitterness which did not subside even after the Nationalists came to power in 1928 and, indeed, survives among some Chinese inside and outside China to this day.

The Japanese provided an even greater spur to nationalism in Asia when they defeated Russia in 1904-5. Although there is doubt whether the impact of this news was as immediate and as widespread throughout Asia as was once thought, there is no doubt that it remained as a source of encouragement to all the nationalist movements of Asia for the next few decades. Most important of all, it heightened the view that the struggle was not merely against any specific Western power, but also against the very idea of Western superiority. The strongest impact of such a view was felt in India and Burma, Indonesia and Vietnam.

In these conquered areas of the British Indian Empire, the Dutch East Indies and French Indo-China, the initial reactions to Western dominance were a number of futile efforts at armed resistance, especially in North-West India, in Upper Burma, in Acheh and in Tongking. All of them reflected the last efforts to defend dynastic and traditional rights rather than the beginnings of a nationalist counter-attack. They were battles against the British, the Dutch or the French. They had not yet drawn anything from the growing awareness that most parts of Asia had been overwhelmed by a superior new civilisation. Also, after conquest, unlike Japan and China, there were no effective local elites left to lead the fight back to positions of equality, dignity and cultural relevance. For such areas, a new kind of strategy had to be devised, and this was largely done by the new Indian elites, especially of Bengal and of the Western cities of Bombay and Madras. They were largely educated in British values and worked comfortably within the British imperial framework. They were aware that the West was superior in many important ways and thought that the British were the most superior of the lot, not least because the British were strong and well-organised in India. For the new Indian elites, there was no question of military salvation or a political *coup d'état* or a long-term economic victory over British capitalists. The nationalists had to fight their war by the rule of law and the use of political ideals implicit in British superiority and by the full exercise of all aspects of civil rights available in India and in Britain. They had learnt readily from the nationalism of the West and sought inspiration from the Irish nationalists, the Boers in South Africa, as well as from the nineteenth-century Italian nationalists. At the same time, they had also sensed the emerging common cause in Asia against Western dominance and found no contradiction between the two. Ultimately, as they led the voices of anti-colonial nationalism, they found men like Gandhi and Nehru to lead them, men who were prepared to mobilise mass support for a broader moral challenge to Western civilisation itself.

This was a long haul, just as long as that which China had to undergo. But, for the Indians as for most other anti-colonial nationalists, there was one important advantage. Their movements were organised within a viable order, beneath an effective bureaucracy and through a steadily developing economy. There was no need for the anarchy and cultural demoralisation that accompanied China's nationalism in the 1910s and 1920s. Even more important, the Indian strategy against colonial rule served as a model for the new nationalist movements which arose in Ceylon, Burma and Indonesia and, to a lesser extent, Vietnam. And in being such a model, it confirmed the view that nationalism in each empire might be directed against a single Western power but that nationalism in Asia was part of a wider concern with restoring all non-Western peoples to political equality in the new world order.

It is true that each group of nationalists was largely confined to fighting its battles against its own imperial master and, until the 1920s, even the strongest group, the nationalists in India, was still relatively weak. A further blow came when it began to appear that Japan had joined the Western supremacists in imperialist activities against Korea, Manchuria and China, albeit in the name of anti-Western nationalism. Was nationalism enough if it tempted successful nationalists to join the ranks of the powerful against other weaker nationalists? Everywhere except in Japan, the nationalists were finding their progress slow. Through the 1920s and 1930s, they were increasingly reminded of the solidarity of the imperial powers in Asia. The era of open rivalry being over, the British, the French, the Dutch and to some extent, even the Americans, did not interfere with one another's efforts to crush their respective nationalists. If anything, they co-operated with and learnt from one another and were anxious when one of them seemed to treat their nationalist leaders too leniently or too harshly. This produced the interaction which kept alive, in both imperial governments and local nationalists, the idea that nationalism was not an isolated phenomenon and could not be confined. It kept alive the idea that nationalism needed help across imperial boundaries if it was to succeed and alerted the Western powers to try and prevent it from doing so as much as they could.

It is in this context that a new and sophisticated analysis of world economic and political forces came to find an audience in Asia. This was the Hobson-Lenin interpretation of Western dominance, especially in Asia and Africa, as being part of the imperialist phase of a mature capitalism. It did not immediately attract the attention of Asian nationalists. It seemed too abstract to be relevant to their local needs. Also, it had unflattering things to say about Asian elites. But when Lenin led the Russian Bolsheviks to victory, the interpretation came to be taken more seriously. And during the 1920s and 1930s, when Soviet and Comintern leaders asserted the thesis with increasing vehemence and conviction, the nationalists in Asia were encouraged by this view. The thesis confirmed that the nationalists were facing a completely new phenomenon. It explained why the Asian nations had, since the nineteenth century, been swamped by forces hitherto unknown and why they were made to feel that Western supremacy was going to be a permanent matter. It was refreshing and reassuring to read in the Hobson-Lenin thesis and the propaganda of communism that this supremacy was the product of objective and impersonal historical forces arising out of industrial capitalism, that further new forces had already been set afoot and that that supremacy was subject to change and was likely to be temporary.

Perhaps not least of the attractions of the thesis and the propaganda was that it shifted the analysis from one emphasising the sense of political and cultural inferiority to one emphasising stages of economic and historical change. The upper and middle class nationalist leaders were not entirely convinced, but they were encouraged by the unexpected support of various kinds of radicals and revolutionaries who conceded that nationalist movements had initially to be led by the bourgeoisie. Those leaders who wondered if nationalism by itself was enough began to ask if it was not necessary to harness some of the ideas, the organisational and propaganda skills of these radicals and revolutionaries, to their nationalist cause. Significantly, a transformed Russia had broken ranks with its former fellow-imperialists and was offering to help anti-Western nationalists. Should the nationalists not accept that help? Sun Yat-sen in China thought they should, and later and to a lesser extent, so did Nehru in India and Sukarno in Indonesia as well as several leading nationalists in Burma and Vietnam. They saw no difficulties in extending their calls for freedom and equality to overlap with issues of economic and social equality. The revolutionaries were told to support the nationalists and the nationalists were strengthened by that support. The nationalists saw no contradiction in this provided they could ensure that their movements were not captured by the revolutionaries.

As it turned out, some of the nationalists who accommodated the communists found that they were wrong. Stalin's failure in China in the late 1920s at least showed that there were contradictions. The nationalism which served as an instrument for attaining political and cultural equality for the new Asian elites could not apparently be reconciled with the nationalism which was being used as a means of achieving international social and economic equality. The Western powers were also quick to alert their nationalists to this contradiction and warn them of the dangers of internationalism to the nationalist cause. And, on the whole, the nationalists took heed. But they did perceive that the Western powers considered the revolutionaries as the bigger long-term threat to their supremacy and had, therefore, become more accommodating to the nationalists. And they also discovered that a concern for internal social and economic growth and welfare need not be tied to socialism or communism, but could easily be fitted into the vocabulary of growth and welfare used in the imperial motherlands of Britain, France, the Netherlands and the United States. This was an important break-through for the nationalist cause. It ceased thereafter to be merely a movement of the upper and middle classes seeking past and present glory. It began to attract greater mass support for throwing out the alien powers and joining in building their own ideal non-exploitative state. The Hobson-Lenin thesis failed to divert the nationalists from their goal, but it certainly enriched their movements, and, by extending their understanding of social and economic factors, helped to ensure their eventual success.

I must be careful not to ignore the most obvious feature of nationalism, its link with the modern nation-state. But it must be pointed out that the significance of this link was not immediately obvious to the early generations of nationalists. It certainly did not play as positive a role in mobilising support as did the calls to defend against and challenge the West and the desire for social and economic change. At times, especially in states which comprised many ethnic groups, the nation-state idea was a distinct obstacle to nationalism. It was not until nationalists were on the point of success that the legal and administrative identity and the territorial limits of the state became outstanding problems. And, in most cases in Asia, it was not until the end of World War II that nationalists faced up to the nuts and bolts questions of how to rule a new nation-state. By that time, they had mostly outgrown their anti-Westernism and brought their social and economic concerns well within the boundaries they inherited.

I have already mentioned the colonial power's preference for dealing with each group of nationalists separately and within the boundaries of the colony concerned. This was partly to make the problem more manageable and partly to counter the common anti-Western nationalism or the internationalist crusade against Western capitalist exploitation. But, more important, this preference was the logical consequence of the meticulous Western concern for the extent and limits of state power. The physical extent and limits were the most obvious and these were determined by the boundaries the imperial power happened to have drawn up. These boundaries tended to become permanent and it became increasingly clear that they would prescribe the limits of any future nation-state. The given shape and size of the future nation-state troubled most nationalists. In all cases, there were majority and minority peoples they had to try and accommodate in one national movement. In many cases, this was achieved temporarily and artificially and with great difficulty. Notable failures were the Hindu extremists who repelled most Muslims in India and the Vietnamese who briefly tried to arouse the Cambodians and Laotians to support an Indo-Chinese nationalist movement. Great difficulties were also encountered by Javanese leaders in the Outer Islands of the Dutch East Indies, the Singhalese in Ceylon and the Burmans in Burma. And particularly artificial were the well-intentioned non-communal nationalist sentiments proclaimed belatedly in the highly fragmented Malay and Bornean states.

Yet the remarkable fact about nationalism in Asia was that, eventually, as it grew strong and confident, it preferred to grow within the colonial boundaries. It was not a matter of convenience; it was not a question of having no choice. What was crucial was that, within those boundaries, the colonial power had erected a state, a legal and administrative entity which worked, an entity which the West had succeeded in identifying with the nation. As nationalists, they felt secure in inheriting such an entity and felt challenged to preserve this entity and make it strong, just and prosperous as the colonial power had never done. No matter how common their cause with other nationalists, no matter how essential was anti-imperialist solidarity, they quickly recognised that the nation-state was vital to their kind of nationalism. They were sworn to defend that political entity until independence and beyond. All the same, we may note that this respect for colonial boundaries as the foundation of nationalism has become so universal a phenomenon (not only in Asia, but in Africa as well) that it should be seen as a generalised response to Western patterns of dominance. It was Western law and bureaucracy which laid the foundations of the state in Asia. It is perhaps fitting that the nationalism which began as anti-Western should end by throwing off Western rule in the name of the most Western institutions of the new order.

I have dwelt long on the nationalism of yesterday and left myself with little time for the nationalism of today. This is probably justified because nationalism in Asia today clearly shows its varied heritage of the past century. We can today identify surviving features of the call to challenge the West. We can recognise the contributions of the various visions of social and economic progress. And in particular we see numerous 'nation-states' earnestly engaged in the exhaustive and agonising task of making nations out of their states. The subject is vast. I cannot hope to do justice to it here and must necessarily be highly selective in what I say. I have therefore concentrated on what I believe are the main patterns today.

There is little today to remind us of the early widespread calls to challenge the West. Two of the challenges, those of the Japanese and the Indians, have petered out. Others like the Indonesians and the Burmese put up supporting performances but were in no position to offer challenges. Only the present Chinese challenge remains and it differs greatly in principle and in quality from the earlier Japanese and Indian ones. Let me try and place this Chinese challenge in perspective, and briefly compare it with the two earlier challenges. The Japanese challenge was, from the start, launched in terms of mastering the essentials of Western civilisation and outdoing the West at its own game. The acquisition of physical power was to be followed by united Asian action to oust the West from Asia. But Japanese imperial ambitions in Asia itself became too obvious, and most Asian nationalists found the idea of Japanese leadership less than convincing. By the time Japan launched its campaign to free Asia for the Asians, they found the Asians divided about whether to accept Japanese help or not. Nevertheless, the fact that the challenge dismembered parts of the four Western empires in South-East Asia for more than three years during World War II was enough to launch the new burst of nationalist activities which ended with independence for almost all of South-East Asia.

The Japanese challenge was eventually beaten back and it became clear that a militarist counter-attack against Western dominance was not likely to succeed and no nationalists in Asia today would support this kind of effort. The Japanese themselves have abandoned it and now concentrate on an economic challenge which shows signs of being far more successful. It remains to be seen if the Japanese will still want to challenge the West on its own, or whether they will mobilise other Asian nations economically tied to Japan to join in concerted efforts to free Asia from Western economic dominance. Significantly two factors have changed. The West is already far less dominant and no such effort may be necessary. Also, other features of nationalism in Asia, the rise of a new kind of Chinese state and the success of the nation-state concept throughout South-East Asia, may now make the question of concerted efforts with Japan completely out of date. It may, however, be too early to say that the Japanese have abandoned altogether their image of themselves as leaders of Asia in the fight back against Western supremacy.

The second challenge to the West was the Gandhian attempt in India to match Western civilisation in spiritual power and even surpass it. Gandhi had admirers all over Asia and the nationalist struggle he led was surprisingly successful, possibly because the British Empire had become entangled in its own grand, liberal and humanitarian claims and Gandhi knew it. But the challenge ended in disaster and the partition of India was a major landmark in the failure of Asian nationalists to offer alternatives to Western political, cultural or even spiritual values. Today Gandhism has barely survived in India and most of what survives is too deeply rooted in the Hindu heritage to have any wide appeal. Thus the nationalism of spiritual rejuvenation has fared no better than that of physical strength. There remains the ideal that Asian traditions must surely have an answer to Western power, but the ideal is feeble in the nationalism of discrete and inviolable nation-states.

The most recent challenge has been that of a Chinese communism. This centres on the idea that the Western civilisation based upon an exploitative capitalist system has begun to decay and that more advanced Western ideas and institutions are now available to overthrow the old hulk altogether. The Chinese further claim that these more advanced forms can be nurtured within Asia (also all over the non-Western world), and, once adapted for local use, will replace the decaying Western values which are corrupting the non-West everywhere. We have yet to see the effect of this moral and ideological challenge, although the social and cultural consequences to China itself have been quite spectacular. But from the earlier examples of the Japanese and Indian challenges, there must be doubts about its eventual success. Three reasons for doubt are noteworthy: firstly, there is no evidence so far that Asian nationalists can really act in concert; secondly, there is a large body of evidence to suggest that Western civilisation is still alert, and, even if sick, has strong recuperative powers; thirdly, in the face of nation-state nationalism throughout Asia, political fragmentation is likely to continue with occasional joint regional efforts, but no agreement on a radical moral and ideological challenge seems likely.

The use of nationalism to challenge the West had its early successes, but its appeal today is limited. Much more positive is the association of nationalism with various visions of social and economic progress. Here there were no diverting calls about challenging the West. The emphasis was on the challenge to the nationalist leadership in each nation to reform or reconstruct the structure of its own society and its way of life along progressive, equitable and even egalitarian lines. This is a major extension of the nationalist goals. In a way, it is a more profound fight back against Western dominance to concentrate on freeing the peoples of Asia from traditional ruling elites, from poverty and ignorance, and arousing them to stand up for themselves.

There are, of course, many visions of such progress and all the viable ones come from the West. And it is a measure of nationalist maturity when nationalists are willing to accept ideas and institutions which benefit their nations no matter what their origins. The main competing visions are represented again by the examples of Japan, India and China. By directly imitating the West in the late nineteenth century, the Japanese took the principles of industrial capitalism in its purest and most confident forms. Their rapid success impressed most other Asians and the main Chinese nationalists followed suit during the first half of the twentieth century. The Chinese then turned out to be far less successful and their new leaders since 1949 have rejected the capitalist model altogether. India, on the other hand, steered a middle course between socialism and planned welfare capitalism. Most other Asian nations today look directly at Western models as well as Japanese, Indian and Chinese versions of them. The rival visions of the future have drawn their respective Western supporters, especially the United States, Britain and Soviet Russia, to extend their rivalry into Asia and many Asian nations have joined in the fight for the visions of progress that they have chosen to adopt.

Such Western rivalries have often had unfortunate consequences for the Asian nations, and the fact that China has set itself up as a model on its own and both Japan and India have been encouraged by the United States and the USSR respectively to compete for influence over the rest of Asia has not made it easier for the nationalists of lesser nations, most notably Vietnam and Cambodia, Pakistan and Bangladesh. It is premature to predict how these ideological pressures on nationalism will affect the future map of Asia. Their main contributions, however, are worth noting. They have kept nationalist leaders on their toes about the need for nationalism to initiate cultural change, to hasten economic growth, to consider questions of social justice, and generally to deliver the goods. Such goals have greatly widened the horizons of the nationalists and freed most of them from both the obsessions about challenging the West and the impractical isolationism of going it alone.

Finally, the most painful part of nationalism, away from anti-Western glory and away from visionary programs of social and economic progress. I refer to the hard task of moulding nations out of the peoples who live in the inherited new states of Asia. Here the problem is least severe in Japan, but almost everywhere else in Asia, the old imperial boundaries as well as the new armistice lines of Korea and Vietnam have marked off nation-states whose primary concern today is to make nations out of their citizens so that they can better defend their sovereignty. The nationalist leaders are not alone in their anxieties about what such tasks entail. The Western powers which helped to create this problem for Asian nationalists are themselves also ambivalent about such nation-state engineering, accompanied as they are both by tragedies and absurdities. They are specially uncertain about the smaller and weaker nation-state whose economy is barely viable and for whom nation-building is expensive and wasteful. In addition, such fragmentary political units are led to build walls against one another, to provide pawns for the larger powers both inside and outside Asia and to be a major source of instability in the world. This is particularly true of South-East Asia and Ceylon, but recent events on the Indian sub-continent suggest that this kind of nation-building will continue to disrupt countries like India, Pakistan and Bangladesh for years to come.

This is, of course, not all negative. The majority peoples in the new nations have benefited greatly from the nation-state principle. Their own identity with their respective states cannot but be an exhilarating one. By the Western principles of nationhood, they seem justified in their pride and act accordingly to press upon their minorities to assimilate and share that pride in national identity. It is probably sheer sentimentality to regret the passing of smaller tribal and ethnic groups into the uniformity of a nation-state. Nevertheless it is necessary to re-affirm that the overwhelming weight of history shows that nation-states are not by definition good and progressive. They can become conservative and even reactionary. All that can be asserted in any definition of the nation-state is that each of them contains land and people and the potential to grow or be reduced in size and numbers and may, in fact, progress or regress in a number of totally different directions. In themselves, without the benefit of significant thought and humanitarian goals, there is ample evidence to show that nation-states are apt to arouse a savage pride, viciously greedy when the states are strong and deeply oppressive to the human spirit when they are weak. The Western powers have had longer experience of the possible political and moral vacuum in this legalistic and jurisdictional frame. During the imperial period there had been concern to provide some modernising content to replace the decadent features of some local traditions before each new state was given its independence. But so many factors intervened, especially in the years immediately after the end of World War II, that this was rarely successful. For one thing, Asian nationalists were suspicious of what Westerners thought was good for them. For another, the pressures towards independence were so great that there was little time to digest what was offered. In addition, no one was really sure of Western sincerity when some of the content was hastily thrust upon the nationalists in terms of the Cold War and the nation-states were suddenly treated like valuable future allies against communism.

The point still has to be made that the nation-state principle was but one and the narrowest of the principles of nationalism in the West itself. Nationalism in the West had arisen out of a common past, and owing to the shared experiences and the many lessons in their history, it had from time to time transcended narrow state loyalties. Its greatest moments were when it put aside its own narrow concerns to regulate international behaviour, to produce scientific and technological innovations together, to deepen and widen the social and cultural heritage and to promote that Western heritage into a new cosmopolitanism for the modern world. Western nationalists themselves realise that whenever they failed to do this and resorted to the narrow exclusive pursuit of their respective self-interests, there was disaster, ranging from the disasters of the two world wars this century to the absurdities of Belgian bilingualism and the tragedies of Northern Ireland. Such experiences confirm that it is no longer necessary, least of all wise, to treat the nation-state features of nationalism as central to that historical phenomenon. If this is not grasped and the exclusiveness of the nation-state is emphasised, then nationalism in Asia is likely to be a dangerously unstable force and a distinct obstacle to whatever kinds of progress the nationalists may claim to want for their peoples.

I do not wish to deny the continued usefulness of the nation-state as a legal entity. The nation-state is probably here to stay for a long time and Asians like other peoples elsewhere will have to learn to live with it. From the relevant parts of the longer Western experience, it would appear that the nation-state as a basic political unit should be ready to co-operate or even act in concert with other similar units as often as possible and its nationals encouraged to contribute beyond its boundaries towards a wider shared heritage. What endangers all nation-states is when they are used mainly as a vehicle for nationalism. Ironically, the continued survival of existing nation-states in Asia (and elsewhere) may actually depend on the decline and even decay of the nationalism which helped to create them.

The history of nationalism in Asia is still brief and whether its future role will be positive or negative is yet uncertain. I suggest that the real challenge to nationalism in Asia lies in what happens to it after the independence of the many nation-states. Following from the aspects that I have discussed, I believe that anti-Western nationalism has perhaps little more to offer Asian nationalists and that the nation-states must act less as instruments for nationalism than as the building blocks for an effective international structure. In particular, the cumulative evidence of nationalism in both the West and in Asia leads me to believe that the wider quest for national progress may, in the long run, be far better made beyond strict national boundaries.

**6**

# Political and Social Aspects of Israeli and Arab Nationalism

*Shlomo Avineri*

In 1905 there appeared in Paris a volume that was to become one of the classical expressions of Arab nationalism. It was written in French, and its author, Neguib Azoury, was like many other early Arab nationalists a Christian Arab. He founded in Paris the Ligue de la Patrie Arabe, whose avowed aim was the liberation, with French assistance, of Syria and Iraq from Turkish Ottoman rule. In his book, the following remarkable passage occurs:

> Two important phenomena, of the same nature and yet antagonistic, manifest themselves nowadays in Turkish Asia but have drawn very little attention to themselves. They are the awakening of the Arab nation and the latent effort of the Jews to reconstitute on a large scale the ancient kingdom of Israel. These two movements are destined to fight each other continually . . . On the final outcome of this struggle may well hinge the destiny of the whole world.[1]

How much more farseeing and realistic this is than the naively harmonistic visions one usually encounters in most of the early Zionist writings. In his *Der Judenstaat,* published in 1896, Herzl, for example, who devotes long chapters to a detailed account of the social organisation of the future Jewish state, has only one short paragraph about its army. The Jewish state, he argues, will be neutral and will have no enemies; hence it would need to have only a small professional army to maintain internal and external security.[2] Unlike Azoury's vision of everlasting strife, Herzl sees no conflict or confrontation in store for the Jewish state.

[1] Neguib Azoury, *Le reveil de la nation arabe,* Paris, 1905, p.v.

[2] Theodor Herzl, *The Jewish State,* trans. Sylvie d'Avigdor, 2nd ed., London, 1934, p. 65.

It is not my intention to discuss here the conflict between the two national movements, the Arab and the Jewish, nor to present a detailed history of their respective development. I shall limit myself to an analysis of two aspects in the intellectual and social structures of the two movements. I have, however, to admit that this account may have a bearing on the possibility of an adequate understanding of the conflict, since what I have to say may also be understood as an attempt to give an answer to what appear to be the reasons for the relative success of one of the two movements concerned in reaching internal integration and withstanding external pressure as against the relative failure of the other to achieve similar ends.

Both Arab and Jewish nationalism originate with the impact of modern, Western enlightenment and secularisation on two ancient and traditional societies. Though there have been Jews and Arabs for centuries and millennia, and in the past both communities expressed their consciousness through the establishment and maintenance of political commonwealths, the emergence of a secular, politically-oriented nationalism among both Arabs and Jews is basically a nineteenth-century phenomenon. It was prompted in both cases by the impact of the West on the traditional religious structures of these two societies: for the Arabs it was the emergence of the West as an intellectual, political and technological challenge to their traditional way of life. It started most dramatically with Napoleon's Egyptian expedition – certainly one of the more bizarre by-products of the French Revolution – and the consequent penetration into the Middle Eastern countries of Western merchants, missionaries and ideas at precisely the time at which the traditional religious legitimacy and political paramountcy of the Ottoman Empire was being undermined.[3]

For the Jewish communities of Eastern and Central Europe, the disintegration of the traditional communal way of life and the emergence of modern, secular nationalisms among the general population posed a number of similar problems of identity, self-consciousness and sheer survival. Both Jewish and Arab nationalism, though drawing on a long national and religious history, are thus the children of Western enlightenment and have to be viewed in this context.

## I

Strangely enough, the major push towards a cultural and national Arab renaissance was given by a group of American Presbyterian missionaries. In 1823, the Boston-based American Board of Commissioners for Foreign

[3] For a masterly account of the complexities involved, see Bernard Lewis, *The Middle East and the West*, London, 1963.

Missions established a mission and a school in Beirut. The original idea
was to have the station in Jerusalem, but for political reasons this became
impossible, and the group had to content itself with the less exalted
venue of Beirut.

From the beginning, the Mission encountered a number of severe
handicaps in its work, which ultimately resulted in a pattern of activity
wholly different from the vast vistas opened at about the same time to
a similar group, also hailing from Boston, in Hawaii. The missionaries
were from the start unable to extend their ministry to the vast majority
of the population which was Muslim; the Turkish authorities, barely
tolerating Western missionaries at all, made it perfectly clear that no
proselytising among Muslims would be allowed. The Jewish communities
were not very receptive, to say the least, to the ministrations of the
Boston Brahmins. This left the missionaries with basically one possible
target: the Christian Arab communities — mainly the Maronites, the
Greek Orthodox and some of the lesser Eastern Rite Christian communities. The function of such missionary activity thus becomes that of
converting to Protestantism Christians of long standing, in fact, members
of Christian churches whose history goes back to the origins of Christianity. Whatever theological problems are raised by such activity need
not detain us here. What is of interest to us is that by extending their
educational and charitable activities to these groups, the missionaries
found themselves involved in a very unusual development; what happened was that to these Christian Arab groups the appeal to secular
Arab consciousness became a real alternative to their ambivalent position as second-class subjects in the Muslim Ottoman Empire. Secular
Arab nationalism also became for the missionaries the only legitimate
way in which they could, albeit indirectly, challenge the religious Muslim nature of a society which they felt had to be saved from whatever
sins the infidels were guilty of inflicting on it. If political allegiance
could be forged on the common Arab cultural base shared by Muslim
and Christian Arab alike, Christian Arabs could become the political
and social equals of Muslims. As the doyen of historians of Arab nationalism, George Antonius, himself a Christian Arab, put it: 'The educational
activities of the American missionaries . . . gave the pride of place to
Arabic . . . In that, they were the pioneers; and because of that, the
intellectual effervescence which marked the first stirrings of the Arab
revival owes most to their labours.'[4]

Modern, secular Arab nationalism thus started, in a way, as an
anti-Turkish, basically anti-Islamic, device supported by American

[4] George Antonius, *The Arab Awakening*, London, 1938, p. 43.

missionaries. As if to symbolise this, the first Arabic book to be printed in Syria was a new Arabic translation of the Bible prepared by the head of the Beirut mission, the Reverend Eli Smith, and printed at the new printing press which the missionaries brought over from a previous base in Malta. This introduction of the printing press into Syria was of tremendous importance, and it was accompanied by the development of a new Arabic fount, which Eli Smith ordered in Leipzig for his press, and which became henceforth known as 'American Arabic'.

The most interesting and influential figure in this whole development was Butrus Bustani, and the shift from cultural to political national self-consciousness is most clearly discernible in his career.[5] Bustani was born in 1818 into a Maronite Christian family and became one of the first Christian Arabs converted to Protestantism by the Beirut mission. Besides co-operating with Eli Smith in his translation of the Bible, Bustani wrote the first history of Lebanon, composed several Arabic grammar books, compiled the first modern Arabic dictionary and published the first Arabic modern encyclopaedia. For a while, in 1857, he functioned as acting U.S. Consul in Beirut. He taught for years in the mission school, and later established the first Arabic secular schools, called 'national schools' *(Madrassah wattaniyah);* he translated numerous European books into Arabic, notably *Robinson Crusoe,* set up his own printing press and publishing house and founded a number of periodicals devoted to Arab cultural themes. With his initiative, the mission established in 1866 the Syrian Protestant College, later to become the American University of Beirut, which was to emerge as, and is until this very day, one of the main intellectual centres of Arab nationalism.

Around 1845 Bustani founded the first Arab literary society, Majma' at-tahdhib. It had fourteen charter members, headed by Bustani: eleven of them were Christian Arabs converted to Protestantism, two were missionaries (Dr Cornelius Van Dyke and Dr Henry de Forest) and one, Nasif al-Yaziji, famous in his own right as one of the most important modern writers in Arabic, was a Maronite who did not embrace Protestantism but was employed as a teacher in one of the mission schools.[6] Within less than two years, the society had about fifty members, none of whom was a Muslim.

[5] For a detailed study of his life and work, see A.L. Tibawi, 'The American Missionaries in Beirut and Butrus al-Bustani', *St Antony's Papers,* XVI, London, 1963, pp. 137-82.

[6] Antonius also mentions (on p. 51) that as early as 1842 a committee was formed to promote the establishment of an Arab literary society: its members were Bustani and three of the missionaries. The evidence about this committee has, however, been recently challenged by Tibawi.

Only in 1857 was there established, also on Bustani's initiative, an Arab Learned Society that had also Muslim and Druze members and thus became the first non-sectarian Arab intellectual society.

A tremendous political impetus was given to the efforts of the group around Bustani and the Beirut mission by the 1860 Lebanese communal riots, in which mainly Maronites and Druzes were involved in a series of mutual massacres. Bustani published numerous impassioned appeals, calling upon the various communities to unite in a non-sectarian patriotism as the only alternative to communal rivalries and mutual bloodletting. Through non-sectarian patriotism, *wattaniyah,* based on their common Arabism, members of the various communities would learn to discover their common cause under the aegis of a non-religious allegiance to the Turkish Empire. Arab national self-consciousness, albeit within the Turkish Empire, was thus raised from a mere particular remedy for the ambivalent position of Christian Arabs within a Muslim realm to a focus for general political allegiance, embracing Muslims, Christians and Druzes alike. Despite this, its main appeal, through the rest of the nineteenth century, remained much stronger to Christian than to Muslim Arabs.

A different source for Arab nationalism is to be found in Egypt, whose semi-autonomous position on the periphery of the Ottoman Empire brought forth what Bernard Lewis has called the only territorial, non-confessional patriotism of the nineteenth century in the Middle East. It was much more centred on Egypt than on the common Arab heritage, and the emergence of Muhammad Ali and his son Ibrahim Pasha as reformers and modernisers greatly enhanced the position of Egypt as an independent entity. Nor was the Egyptian regime averse, throughout the nineteenth century, to extending asylum if not outright assistance to various Syrian and Lebanese intellectuals, again mostly Christians, who were calling for an Arab cultural and political renaissance in the lands still under direct Ottoman rule. This became entangled with the movement for Islamic reform: while such reformers as Jamal ad-Din al-Afghani called for a purification of Islam in a way that became very easily utilised by the Pan-Islamic notions of the Ottoman Caliphate, a different development took place in Egypt. While reformers like Muhammad Abdu' were of extreme importance, for our purposes the most significant development was the one heralded by Abdul Rahman al-Kawakibi, a Syrian Muslim who found refuge in Egypt and who evolved a concept of Islamic reform and purification based on the restoration of its pristine Arabic character. In his *The Excellences of the Arabs* (1901), al-Kawakibi argued the reasons which make the Arabs, rather than the Turks, the legitimate rulers of Islam. As against the pro-Ottomanism implied in al-Afghani's Pan-Islamism, al-Kawakibi argued that only the Arabs can truly represent Islam in its purity; he enumerated twenty-six reasons for arguing Arab superiority over any other nation and especially over the Turks. Despite this strong blend of Islam and Arabism, al-Kawakibi also called for the separation of religion and state and thus qualifies, in Sylvia Haim's opinion, as the first intellectual precursor of modern, secular Pan-Arabism:[7] he also prefigures some of the inherent ambiguities of the relationship between Arab nationalism and Islam.

The major transition, however, from the cultural to the political realm occurred in the aftermath of the 1908 revolution of the Young Turks. For the Arabic-speaking population of the Ottoman Empire, this revolution signified not so much the attempt to modernise the Empire as a conscious effort at political centralisation, shifting political allegiance from its Islamic base to an emphasis on the Empire being predominantly a Turkish one. What to the outsider appeared as sensible centralisation and modernisation, to the Arab population manifested itself as the imposition of a conscious, ethnic Ottomanisation. So long as the Empire was conceived as one of the successive Muslim Caliphates, it did not basically present a problem to the allegiance of its Muslim population. But once the ethnic Turkish element came to the fore, the Muslim Arabs, already aroused to a consciousness of their linguistic, ethnic and historical tradition through half a century of cultural revival from Bustani to al-Kawakibi, found themselves for the first times at loggerheads with the Turkish rulers who appeared now as foreign masters and enslavers rather than as co-religionists.[8]

Turkish nationalism itself was, of course, as recent a nineteenth-century phenomenon as Arab nationalism. Originally, it was fostered by groups basically marginal to the ruling elite of the Ottoman Empire. Among its sources were Crimean Tartar refugees who fled in the early nineteenth century to Constantinople in the wake of the Russian annexation of the Crimea and what was later to become South Russia. It is among them that one finds for the first time the emergence of an ethnic

[7] Sylvia G. Haim, ed., *Arab Nationalism*, Berkeley and Los Angeles, 1962, p. 27. For al-Kawakibi's 26 points of excellence of the Arabs, see ibid., pp. 78-80. On the complex relationship between Islam and Arab nationalism, see Sylvia G. Haim's 'Islam and the Theory of Arab Nationalism', in Walter Z. Laqueur, ed., *The Middle East in Transition*, London, 1958, pp. 280-307. See also Nadav Safran, *Egypt in Search of Political Community*, Cambridge, Mass., 1961.

[8] See C. Ernest Dawn, 'From Ottomanism to Arabism', *Review of Politics*, XXIII, 1961, pp. 378-400.

self-consciousness calling for the unification of all Turkic-speaking peoples. Another source, no less interesting, was a number of Polish and Hungarian 1848 refugees who found asylum and employment in the Ottoman Empire which was only too glad to use them as military advisers. Some of them converted to Islam and reached very high positions in the army and administration. The most interesting among them was Count Konstantyn Borzecki, a Polish 1848 refugee, who embraced Islam and became quite prominent in the Ottoman administration as Mustafa Jelaleddin Pasha (his son, Enver, became a member of the Imperial Ottoman General Staff under the Young Turks). In 1869 Jelaleddin published in Constantinople a volume entitled *Les Turcs anciens et modernes,* in which he argued that the Turks are fundamentally a white, European people and the Empire should become a focal point for all Turkic-speaking peoples in South Russia and Central Asia. Others wrote in a similar vein. The most famous European Turcologist of the century, Arminius Vambéry, a Hungarian of Jewish origin, lived for several years in Constantinople and also contributed to the growing awareness of Turkish ethnicity among the young intellectuals of the period who began to style themselves 'Young Ottomans'.[9]

The Young Turks' attempt at Ottomanisation exacerbated reactions among the Arab elite on account of the suspicion that the Committee of Union and Progress, as the Young Turks' high command was known, was also favouring Jewish immigration into Palestine. The fact that Cavid Bey, the Minister of Finance in the CUP cabinet, was a member of the Sabbataean crypto-Jewish sect of the Dönme, gave rise to all kinds of rumours about the contacts between the Zionists and the Young Turks, culminating in some quite absurd speculations about the Jewish origins of the whole Young Turk elite.[10]

But this was mainly a side issue. What we do find is growing resentment against Ottomanisation, and in the years between 1908 and 1914 a number of Arab political organisations spring up expressing the radicalisation of political sentiment among the Arabic-speaking population of the Empire. The Ottoman Decentralisation Party (Hizb al-Lamarkaziya al-Idariya al-Uthmani) was formed around groups in Damascus, Tripoli,

[9] Bernard Lewis, *The Emergence of Modern Turkey,* London, 1961, pp. 339-40. See also Serif Mardin, *The Genesis of Young Ottoman Thought,* Princeton, 1962; and Uriel Heyd, *The Foundations of Turkish Nationalism,* London, 1950.

[10] Neville Mandel, 'Turks, Arabs and Jewish Immigration into Palestine 1882-1914', *St Antony's Papers,* XVII, 1965, esp. pp. 96-7. See also Richard Lichtheim, *Shear Yashuv,* Tel Aviv, 1954, pp. 198-200, 238-40 (in Hebrew); and Sa'adia E. Weltmann, 'Germany, Turkey and the Zionist Movement', *Review of Politics,* XXIII, 1961, pp. 246-69.

Beirut, Jaffa and Jerusalem, calling for a greater measure of autonomy
in the various provinces of the Ottoman Empire. A more radical group,
the Young Arab Society (Jami'at al-Arabiya al-Fatat), was formed in
1911 in Paris with an outspoken political nationalist program. During
World War I, many of the founding members of these organisations
were hanged by the Turks as traitors and the British-inspired Arab revolt
in the desert, so much over-romanticised by T.E. Lawrence, did in fact
cash in on the anti-Turkish feelings of the nationally self-conscious
young Arab intelligentsia in Syria, Palestine and Iraq.

For though in its later stages Arab nationalism became basically anti-
Western and as such found temporary allies first in Nazi Germany and
later in Soviet Russia,[11] its initial political manifestations usually
favoured the British and the French as allies in the ousting of the Turks.
What was sown by the American Presbyterian missionaries of Beirut
was later reaped, in a way, by the British imperial interests which viewed
Arab nationalism as a convenient instrument in their anti-Turkish policies during World War I and later.[12]

One of the intriguing aspects of this development is that while
modern Arab nationalism, with all its ambivalence about the West,
initially welcomed, for political reasons, the Western intrusion into the
Turkish Empire, the most ferocious anti-Western opposition came not
from nationalist but from fundamentalist religious ideologies. Abdul
Kadr in North Africa, the Mahdi in Sudan, the Senoussis in Libya —
these were the forces that were trying to stem the French, British and
Italian incursion into the Arab world. The fact that the only truly
national leader Palestinian Arabs ever had, Hajj Amin al-Husseini, was
Mufti of Jerusalem and raised the holy sites of Islam in Jerusalem to
national symbols, is also very much within this tradition, and the emergence of such fiercely nationalist and anti-Western leaders as Kaddafi
and Boumedienne, who turn to Islam as their basic ideological framework, is of immense significance in assessing the nature of Arab nationalism and its development.

Let us now turn to the origins of modern Jewish nationalism. Enlightenment and secularisation changed radically the conditions of life
of the Jewish communities in Eastern and Central Europe. So long as

[11] President Sadat of Egypt is a case in point. In his autobiography he tells
how, in 1940, when Rommel was at the gates of Alexandria, he and other members of the 'Free Officers' group sought and established contact with Nazi and
Fascist agents against the common British enemy. See Anwar es-Sadat, *Revolt on
the Nile*, London, 1957, pp. 34ff.

[12] For subsequent developments, see Elie Kedourie, 'Pan Arabism and British
Policy', in Laqueur, *The Middle East in Transition*, pp. 100-11.

the Jews had lived as a religious community within the *natio Christiana,* there was ultimately very little ambivalence in their basic condition of existence, whatever difficulties and persecutions they had to endure. They were living in society but were not members of it: a situation acceptable at root both to them and to Gentile society. Thus they were able to maintain their identity through generations of sometimes quite violent persecutions; their marginality turned the walls of the ghetto into a protective coating. In a social order based on hierarchy and distinctions, their apartness was very much in tune with the general *mores* of society.

But the ideas of equal rights brought in by the emancipation and the emergence of modern nationalism in Europe opened a whole set of Pandora's boxes: if Jews were equal to other members of society, should they be allowed to retain their own exclusive customs? Was a Yiddish-speaking Jew from the Pale of Settlement really an equal member of the Polish nation? Could an orthodox Jew really be in communion with republican Frenchmen? Similar questions began to be asked a century later in Arab countries, with the emergence of modern Arab nationalism in Iraq, Egypt, Syria and Morocco; the plight of European Jews in the nineteenth century repeated itself in the Arab world in the twentieth — the anti-Jewish riots in Baghdad during Rashid Ali al-Kailany's nationalist regime in the early 1940s follow similar developments in Eastern Europe half a century earlier.

The emerging first generation of secularly educated and emancipated Jews was thus faced with a set of agonising problems wholly unprecedented in Jewish history. If one does not believe any more in the Jewish orthodox way of life, what, then, is one? Is one really a German? But then the 'real' German, even if emancipated, was a Christian — as shown by Bruno Bauer's argument that Jews could be granted equal rights only if they were converted first and *then* rejected Christianity like the emancipated Christian Germans themselves. Or could one really identify with the Polish nation without relating to Catholicism or with Mother Russia without being a member of the Russian Orthodox Church? In some countries, like certain areas of Poland and Hungary, the Jews were caught in the crossfire, as their emancipation usually took the form of assimilating to Russian and German, rather than to Polish and Magyar, cultures and they found that emancipation turned them into strangers. The leaders of the Jewish Sanhedrin convened by Napoleon must have been less than candid when they declared, under Imperial pressure, that they felt more in common with their Gentile French compatriots than with their co-religionists in other countries. The problem of identity, which in a way never presented itself to Jews leading a traditional life within a Christian, or for that matter Muslim, society, became an excruciating challenge to the modern, secularised Jew. Add to this the breakdown of the old economic order in which Jews had found for themselves a traditional niche in Eastern European society, and one gets a glimpse of the enormous upheavals Jewish communities were undergoing in the nineteenth century.

Many turned to baptism, not always out of religious conviction but, as Heine put it, to gain 'a passport to European culture' or, like Marx's father, to be able to pursue one's career in a secularised society; others found a way out of their predicament in Reform Judaism which postulated that the ethnic elements in Judaism were outdated and tried to forge a Jewish 'confession' in the image of enlightened Protestantism; still others identified with the national and social struggles of their countries, sometimes oblivious to the fact that their participation might hamper the causes they believed in – as in the accusations brought forth first by the Czarist regime and later by the Nazis that socialism and communism are *verjudet;* millions migrated to America and other Western countries. A small minority turned to the secular and cultural aspects of Jewish history in order to find in them a modern, non-religious focus for their identity as Jews.

It is out of these efforts, produced by the ambiguities of the position of the modern, secularised Jew, that there emerged the nineteenth-century revival of Hebrew literature. It is from a combination of Herderianism and classicism that one discovers people turning to Hebrew as a medium of intellectual communication among those Jews who left the ghetto and its religion behind them and yet felt themselves to be Jewish. If there can be Italian and Polish and Czech literature, why not a renaissance of Hebrew? It was German- and Russian-educated intellectuals, not the rabbis in the Pale, who started the revival of Hebrew language and Jewish historical consciousness. It was in Vilna, the crossroads of Polish, Russian and Lithuanian culture, with German always as a *Kultursprache* in the background, that Avraham Mapu wrote the two first modern Hebrew prose novels, *Ahavat Zion* and *Ashmat Shomron;* the Italian Risorgimento prompted the revival of Hebrew poetry and philosophy in Italy under Moshe Chaim Luzzato and Shmuel David Luzzatto; a modern Jewish historiosophy, trying to adapt Hegelian schemes to Jewish history, was first suggested by the Galician-born Nachman Krochmal in his *Guide to the Contemporary Perplexed (Moreh Nevuchei Ha-Zman),* and a student of German historicism, Heinrich Graetz, wrote the first modern history of the Jewish people.

It is among these secularised, Westernised Jewish intellectuals that one finds the emergence of modern Jewish nationalism; the rabbis and the traditionalists were sceptical if not outright hostile to what appeared to them as a secular political creed contravening the traditional religious quietism associated with orthodox Jewish beliefs in messianism. Who could better epitomise the flower of Central European *Kultur* than journalists like Herzl and Nordau, who was more imbued with the European socialist ideas than the early socialist Zionists? It is as a protest against the failure of the naïve belief in emancipation that modern Jewish nationalism appears in the nineteenth century.[13] Nazism was merely the final and most brutal blow dealt to the dream of emancipation as far as Central and Eastern Europe were concerned.

## II

Both Jewish and Arab nationalism had to contend not only with problems of national identity and survival, but were also confronted immediately with enormous issues of social structure. It will be my contention in the remainder of this account that while Jewish nationalism was relatively successful in imbuing its ideology and praxis with a vision of social transformation, Arab nationalism remained mainly political and by ignoring the social dimension was unable to achieve a degree of social cohesion comparable to the one achieved in the social structures of Israel.

Let us start with the problems of Jewish social structure first. What one discerns quite early in Jewish national writings of the nineteenth century is an awareness of the lopsided nature of the Jewish social structure. Jews, it was argued, are to be found almost exclusively in positions of social mediation, be it economic or intellectual; from *this* point of view the social structure of the Pale of Settlement did not differ much from that of the emancipated, Westernised Jewish communities, though the exact roles of Jews changed considerably. There were almost no Jews to be found in primary production – there was no Jewish peasantry, hardly any Jewish proletariat (in so far as one found a Jewish proletariat in some urban Polish areas towards the end of the nineteenth century it was in the unique conditions in which Jewish economic urban development was quicker than that of the general society: a development which itself contributed to antisemitism both among the Gentile middle class and among the Gentile proletariat). A Jewish renaissance, so it was argued, would have to be accompanied by a conscious realignment of the social structures of Jewish society. The

[13] See Arthur Hertzberg, ed., *The Zionist Idea*, New York, 1960; Ben Halpern, *The Idea of the Jewish State*, Cambridge, Mass., 1961.

Return to Zion would not have to be a mere territorial shift in population: in order to be successful, it would have to be accompanied by the development of a Jewish peasantry and a Jewish working class.

The development of these ideas can be traced most dramatically in the career of Moses Hess, Marx's mentor and his so-called 'communist rabbi', who is also considered as one of the founding fathers of socialist Zionism. He now lies buried in the first kibbutz on the shores of the Sea of Galilee, but he was initially interred in a Cologne cemetery under a tombstone carrying the inscription *Vater der deutschen Sozialdemokratie.* His private papers are to be found divided between the Central Zionist Archives in Jerusalem and the Institute for Marxism-Leninism in Moscow, and editions of his works are being published by the Zionist Library in Jerusalem and the Academy of Sciences of the German Democratic Republic. He deserves a much closer study than the few footnotes usually referring to him as an 'influence' or 'forerunner'.

Though only six years older than Marx, Hess was born into a strictly Orthodox Jewish family in the Rhineland, while Marx grew up in a family that had been baptised. Unlike Marx who had no Jewish education and knew practically nothing about Judaism, Hess's only education had been a Jewish religious one. It was said of him that he belonged to that generation of Jews who learned their German from studying Hegel and their Latin from studying Spinoza.

Like many of his generation, Hess reacted most strongly against his Orthodox upbringing. His repudiation of Judaism became total and fierce. In his first book, *The Holy History of Mankind,* Hess refers to two nations of 'world historical importance' which are nowadays lifeless cadavers: the Jews and the Chinese. Following a somewhat simplified version of Hegel's philosophy of history, Hess characterises the Jewish people as 'spirit without body' and the Chinese as 'body without spirit'. Judaism's role in history has been completed and though the Jews may experience a revival it will be as individuals totally immersed in universal Western culture. Spinoza is to Hess an example of this new type of Jew who transcends the narrow limits of his origins and merges into the universal spirit – his anonymous book actually gives 'a Young Spinozist' as author.

The last chapter of the volume is indeed called 'The New Jerusalem': in it Hess paints a picture of a future society organised in communes, in which distinctions between town and country, as well as between man and woman, would disappear. But 'it is in the heart of Europe that this New Jerusalem will be founded'.[14]

In an unpublished draft written around 1840 and called *The Poles and the Jews,* Hess says that one may expect a renaissance among both the Poles and the Jews, but while the Polish renaissance will be political, the Jewish one will be purely spiritual. The Jews lack the two basic conditions for national life, territory and language; they have repeatedly shown a total lack of national consciousness *(Mangel an Nationalsinn).* Even traumatic experiences like the Damascus Affair have failed to arouse in them a sense of cohesion, and they are destined to disappear as a separate group through assimilation and integration into the new Europe of the spirit.[15] Similarly in his *European Triarchy* Hess suggests that through their rejection of Jesus, the Jews have become a 'mummy'.[16] And in his essay *On the Essence of Money,* Hess identifies Judaism and the cult of money — an identification which was later taken over and elaborated by Marx in his *On the Jewish Question.*[17]

We thus see that though the Jewish question comes up quite frequently in Hess's writings, and his well-informed historical account of early Judaism unmistakably shows the signs of his religious schooling, his attitude to Judaism is basically hostile and if he had a message to deliver it is that of total assimilation and ultimate disappearance.

Almost twenty years later, however, Hess experiences a complete transformation of his views on the subject. In 1862 he publishes his *Rome and Jerusalem,* which he originally intended entitling 'The Rebirth of Israel'. In the Preface he very much takes up the posture of the prodigal son:

> Here do I stand, after an estrangement of twenty years, in the midst of my people. Only one thought, which I felt I had stifled forever in my breast, presents itself vividly before my eyes: the thought of my nationality, which cannot be separated from the heritage of my forefathers, the Holy Land and the Eternal City, the birthplace of the belief in unity of the divine and the future brotherhood of all men.[18]

[14] [Moses Hess], *Die heilige Geschichte der Menschheit,* Stuttgart, 1837, pp. 339-40, 80, 308.

[15] MS. A49/8 in the Zionist Central Archives, Jerusalem.

[16] Moses Hess, *Die europäische Triarchie,* Leipzig, 1841, p. 112.

[17] For this and other details of Hess's life, Edmund Silberner's definitive biographical study, *Moses Hess: Geschichte seines Lebens,* Leiden, 1966, should be consulted. The best English résumé of Hess's works is to be found in Isaiah Berlin's 'The Life and Opinions of Moses Hess', in Philip Rieff, ed., *On Intellectuals,* Garden City, N.Y., 1970, pp. 137-82.

[18] *Roma und Jerusalem,* in Moses Hess, *Ausgewählte Schriften,* ed. Horst Lademacher, Köln, 1962, p. 228.

The book is written as a series of letters to a fictional lady correspondent, and Hess finishes one of the letters with a highly emotional outburst that he is happy to revert to his original name Moses and discard his adopted name of Maurice, further commenting: 'I only regret that I cannot be called Itzig'.[19]

How may one account for such a complete change of attitude? On the evidence of Hess's own account of his conversion, there had been a number of reasons: the success of Italian nationalism, which became a great triumph for the European Left, was certainly one of the main driving forces; the Rome in the title of the book is Mazzini's *Roma terza,* though the overtones of Rome of the Pagan Emperors and the Catholic Popes are, of course, also evident. Whereas for Marx national unity was viewed purely as instrumental (it helps the working class to focus on its true class interest), Hess followed Mazzini in arguing that the nation is a community in which individuals transcend their pure egotism and it is on its foundations that a socialist international 'community of communities' would be established.

Hess also cites as a reason for his advocacy of Jewish nationalism the increasingly racialist overtones of European, and particularly, German nationalism: in this he is one of the first to discern the catastrophic consequences of the failure of liberal nationalism in Germany in 1848. German nationalism, Hess argues, is becoming xenophobic, militaristic and racist, and there is no hope for the Jews of incorporation into the New Germany.

Another formative influence Hess mentions is a volume by a French radical, Ernest Laharanne: *La nouvelle question d'Orient.* Laharanne became greatly disturbed by the communal riots in Lebanon in 1860 (the same riots which we saw so instrumental in politicising Butrus Bustani's thought). He saw in them an ultimate proof of the bankruptcy of the Ottoman Empire: France, he argues, true to its revolutionary tradition of supporting enslaved peoples against their oppressors, should now espouse the cause of the new nationalisms in the Levant. In place of the old Ottoman Empire, Laharanne sees the emergence of two Arab states, one in Syria-Mesopotamia and the other in Egypt. In the area between the two he envisages the formation of a new Jewish state, and he calls upon France to help establish 'les empires d'Egypte et d'Arabie et la réconstitution de la nation juive'.

But beyond all these motives, the prime force in Hess's argument is that emancipation has not worked. Bourgeois society has not been able

---

[19] Ibid., p. 250.

to solve the Jewish problem, and because of this the Jews in bourgeois society have been put into invidious positions which made their integration in a future socialist society in Europe quite impossible. Reform Judaism failed similarly; not only did it, according to Hess, emasculate historical Judaism, but also, by stressing the purely confessional rather than the national aspect of Judaism, it substituted the eternal Jewish dream of communal redemption for the Christian message of merely individual salvation.

In his historical account of Judaism in *Rome and Jerusalem* Hess similarly takes a completely different attitude from the one that informed his early writings, where Judaism had been associated with the cult of money. This may or may not be the case of the Jews in the Diaspora: Judaism as a system of social ethics, both in biblical and talmudic times, is portrayed by Hess as a proto-socialist system.

The romantic idealisation here is obvious, but the examples are nonetheless illuminating. Jewish sabbatarian legislation is portrayed as socially motivated, as the first historical instance of social legislation in which even slaves were included. Judaism, Hess argues in a letter dating from the same period, knows no classes, has no feudalism, is basically 'social democratic'.

The Jewish family figures quite prominently in this historical account: the family and not the individual has always been, according to Hess, the focus of Jewish life. 'Judaism never severed the individual from the family, nor the family from the nation, nor the nation from humanity.'[20] The family appears here, in a Hegelian fashion, as a community, in contradistinction to what Hess sees as the fundamental individualism of Christian society. Moreover, whereas Gentile society, be it pagan or Christian, worshipped masculinity and its attributes, in Judaism it was the feminine virtues of compassion, suffering, love and understanding, associated with the Jewish mother, that were always dominant: 'every Jewish mother is a *mater dolorosa*'. On the evidence of a paragraph in the talmudic tractate *Pirkei Avoth* ('Ha-omer sheli sheli v-shelcha shelcha, zo mida beinonit, ve-yesh omrim zo midat Sdom') Hess concluded that 'the ordinary bourgeois morality of *chacun pour soi* is alien to Judaism'.[21]

But Judaism, Hess contends, cannot be rejuvenated in the Diaspora, and certainly not in bourgeois society: the Jewish masses will be able to participate 'in the great movement of modern mankind' only when they will have a Jewish homeland, when they will be engaged, like any other nation, in primary production.

[20] Ibid.

[21] Ibid., p. 233.

It is indeed to the Jewish 'masses', that is the populace of Eastern European Jewry, and not to the assimilated Western Jew that Hess turns his attention; there, Jewish consciousness is still alive, there suffering is quite brutal, and it will be from there that the immigration to Palestine will come. It will be the impoverished *Ost-Juden* and the Middle Eastern Sephardim that will make up the bulk of the population of the new society. It is among these communities that the traditional communal spirit of Judaism is still alive, whereas Western Jews have been corrupted by individualism. Hess has, for example, a great, and somewhat naïve, admiration for Hassidism: while criticising what he calls its 'religious superstitions', he sees in its way of life a communal togetherness, transcending individual atomism.

With such a background, Jewish immigration to the Land of Israel will not, in Hess's opinion, create another free-enterprise society. The new society will be organised 'according to Mosaic, i.e. socialist, principles', there will be no private property in land, agricultural settlements will be formed on a communal basis, industry and commerce will be likewise organised according to co-operative principles. The New Jerusalem will be a socialist Jewish society.

Just as the national liberation of Italy and Poland became a central cause for the nineteenth-century European Left, so the solution of 'the last nationality problem' should be espoused by European socialists. Hess's latter-day Jewish nationalism was not a reversal from early socialist principles, though it obviously involved a change of heart about the Jewish question. The recent East German editors of Hess usually ignore his Zionism, briefly referring to it in one instance as an aberration, an inexplicable throw-back to 'the religion of his youth'. This is obvious nonsense, since Hess is not reverting to Jewish religious orthodoxy but is trying to evolve a concept of Jewish nationalism, and the future Jewish commonwealth envisaged by Hess is postulated in socialist terms.

Despite all the romanticisation involved in the Zionist socialist attempt to create a Jewish peasantry and a Jewish working class in Palestine, this ultimately proved to be the main reason for the ability of the new society to maintain itself. Zionism thus became the only migration movement with *a conscious ideology of downward social mobility*. While all the great mass migration movements of the nineteenth century were motivated by the promise of upward social mobility — and this includes, of course, the three million Jewish immigrants from Czarist Russia to the West during the 1882-1914 period — the handful of Zionist immigrants to the Land of Israel were mainly middle and lower middle class people who went to the New Zion in order to become labourers and peasants and thus lay the foundations for a new type of Jewish social structure.

Though much of this initial ideology is not as evident today in Israel as it was years ago, it was responsible for the creation of the basic socio-economic structures which characterise Israeli society until this day. The emergence of the *kibbutz* and the *moshav* as forms of collective and co-operative organisation, the fact that most of the land is publicly owned, the hegemony of the labour movement in Israel's life and the fact that all Israeli governments have been headed by the Labour Party, the evolution of the *Histadruth* not only as a merely powerful trade union organisation but also as a Labour-owned section of industry, the fact that the commanding heights of the Israeli economy are publicly owned — all these, together with the basic egalitarianism of Israeli society, are elements that can be traced back to the combination of national ideology and social critique leading to the social vision implied in Zionism.

Though Hess was the first to evolve this combination of Zionism and socialism, he was less influential, in the long run, than some later, perhaps less original minds. Mention should be made of only two of them, signifying the different streams of thought that went into Labour Zionism. One was Aharon David Gordon, who under the influence of Tolstoyan ideals became an agricultural labourer at a very advanced age and in his writings extolled the idea of 'the religion of labour', suggesting that physical labour should become part of the life experience of every individual, and especially of intellectuals. The other was Dov Ber Borochov, whose amalgam of Plekhanovite Marxism and Zionism was perhaps the most influential in the emergence of Labour Zionism in Israel.[22]

What is interesting is that this awareness of the social dimension in Zionism appears even in the writings of those Zionist thinkers who cannot be called socialists. Herzl represents the liberal, bourgeois element in Zionist thought, yet even he refers on the first page of the Preface to *Der Judenstaat* to Thomas More's *Utopia* and to the popular utopian novel *Freiland* by his Viennese contemporary, the economist Theodor Hertzka.[23] The social structure of Herzl's *The Jewish State* envisages, among other features, public ownership of land and a seven-hour working day. When Herzl came up with a flag for the new state,

[22] Ber Borochov, *Nationalism and the Class Struggle: a Marxian Approach to the Jewish Problem*, ed. Abraham G. Duker, New York, 1937, esp. pp. 183-205.

[23] Hertzka was an academic economist who wrote his socialist utopia largely under the influence of what he considered to have been Marx's main achievement in being the first 'to proclaim the connection between the problem of value and modern capitalism'. See his *Freeland*, trans. Arthur Ransom, London, 1891, p. xxi.

he suggested an arrangement of seven golden stars on a white field, for 'it will be under the banner of labour' that the Jews will return to their land.[24] A few years later Herzl wrote a utopian novel, *Altneuland*, clearly modelled on Hertzka's *Freiland*, in which the new Jewish society in Palestine is based on Proudhonist mutualist principles. Like many other utopian novels, Herzl's abounds with long didactic speeches about the new life, in this case hailing Mutualism as the realisation of social justice and the abolition of the power of privately owned capital.

## III

Arab society, on approaching and achieving political independence, was faced with a similar problem of social structure. While it can be said of Jewish society that in the nineteenth century it was almost exclusively middle class, Arab Muslim society hardly had a middle class for a number of historical reasons. It is my argument that Arab nationalism remained almost exclusively political, had very little to say about the problem of social structures and hence was almost completely unsuccessful in effecting the transformation of Arab society that would have been necessary for political independence to be more than a hollow crown.

As the previous remarks on Arab nationalism pointed out, the Arabs lived for centuries under foreign rule before the British and the French moved into the area. Before the establishment of Western paramountcy in the Middle East, Arab society was not a self-governing entity. Ever since the twelfth century, the Arabic-speaking population of the Middle East was ruled by a succession of foreign invaders: first the Crusaders, later the Muslim Seljuks, Tartars, Osmanli Turks, Mameluke slaves (in Egypt). It is the Islam of all of these conquerors, except the Crusaders, which gave them, as we have seen, legitimacy in Arab consciousness. But socially speaking the consequence was that the political elites in Arab societies were not Arabs but members of a foreign ethnic and linguistic group. Arab society, on achieving independence, had hardly a traditional political elite of its own.

Furthermore, because of Islamic precepts and the nature of the Arab Muslim *Conquista* of the Middle East in the seventh century, Muslim Arab society looked with disdain on commercial activity: mercantile activity was never considered to be the right thing for a true Muslim to be engaged in. As a consequence, most of the urban mercantile middle classes in Arab society in the nineteenth and twentieth centuries turned out to be composed of non-Muslim minority groups: Christian Arabs, Armenians, Greeks, Jews. The

---

[24] *The Jewish State*, p. 65 — the English translation mistakenly writes 'honour' instead of 'labour'.

Christian Arabs, as we have seen, had been crucial in the initial steps of Arab nationalism (they still figure very strongly among the most radical nationalist groups: most of the membership of the Popular Front for the Liberation of Palestine comes from among Christian Arabs), but they could not give the movement its social backbone.

Thus Arab society lacked a Muslim Arab middle class, so central to formative stages of nationalism, and it was this gap in the social structure which was responsible for the breakdown of the democratically-oriented constitutions which most Arab countries adopted on achieving independence.

There has been very little in Arab nationalist literature about the need to overhaul the existing social structure. Arab nationalism has been generally focusing its attention on political aims, and there has been no preoccupation parallel to the one which characterised Zionism on the need to transform society as well. This purely political conception of nationalism usually viewed an external political enemy as being responsible for the woes of Arab society; first it was the Turkish Empire, then British and French and Western imperialism in general, now it is the existence of Israel. The degree of self-criticism that went along with Jewish nationalism, the consciousness that political goals by themselves are not enough, never had its counterpart in Arab nationalism.

Hence the role of the army in present-day Arab societies: the army entered into politics not because it was the most modernising element in society; in a way it is that sector of society which has been exposed more than other sectors of society to Western influence on a technological level. But this did not change its basically conservative social structure, nor did it deprive it of something else which is crucial to its role in society: within Islam, and in Arab society in particular, there is a basic legitimacy to military rule. This goes back both to the ethos of Islam as a religion of conquest, and also to the fact that the historical structures of Arab societies after Islam have all been based on the rule of a military elite. There never was in Arab society the ambiguity characterising Western societies, as well as Indian society, about military rule. Interestingly enough, there has never arisen in any of the Arab countries now under military rule an opposition to the very idea of the army being the dominant element in politics. There may be criticism of this or that policy of any given military regime, there is certainly opposition to the rule of this or that military group or military leader, but the sort of basic opposition to the very idea of military rule, which one finds in almost any Western society that came under a military dictatorship, is quite lacking in Arab society.

Not one Arab intellectual voice has been raised in protest against it as a matter of principle. In this, Arab society is quite reminiscent of the Latin American tradition of the army in politics; after all, they both have a military conquest as their origin.

As Bernard Lewis pointed out, modernisation in the Arab world was usually tried through the introduction of new techniques into the army. But it is here that the crisis of modernisation became most felt in Arab society: one cannot modernise a society by modernising its army, and one cannot achieve a modern army unless one modernises society from the bottom up. This is the vicious circle in which so many Arab societies find themselves at the moment: whatever one may say about the Egyptian army, for example, it is not that it does not have modern techniques of organisation and warfare at its disposal. As a matter of fact, the Egyptian army has been undergoing modernisation since the days of Muhammad Ali, though the nationality and politics of the foreign instructors have changed over the generations. If its performance is still problematic, it is not the fault of the army, nor is it to be ascribed to the instructors. The fault goes back to the social structures on which the army is based.

Engels, who was keen on military matters, observed an analogous phenomenon when discussing the nineteenth-century Persian army:

> The fact is that the introduction of European military organisation with barbaric nations is far from being completed when the new army has been subdivided, equipped and drilled after European fashion. . . The main point, and at the same time the main difficulty, is the creation of a body of officers and sergeants, educated on the modern European system, totally freed from the old national prejudices and reminiscences in military matters, and fit to inspire life into the new formation. This requires a long time, and is sure to meet with the most obstinate opposition from Oriental ignorance, impatience, prejudice, and the vicissitudes of fortune and favour inherent to Eastern courts.[25]

It is true that the last decade has seen a remarkable rise in the intensity of radical social ideologies in the Middle East.[26] Very little of this has spilled over into praxis, and the entrenched social class interests of the military elite have been one of the main obstacles in this direction. But even on the ideological level one would be hard

[25] 'Persia-China', *New York Daily Tribune*, 5 June 1857, in Karl Marx, *On Colonialism and Modernization*, ed. Shlomo Avineri, Garden City, N.Y., 1968, p. 177.

[26] See Leonard Binder, *The Ideological Revolution in the Middle East*, New York, 1964.

pressed to find any comprehensive view of social transformation which manages to overcome the purely political aims common to the various trends of Arab nationalism. Not that on the purely political level one can really find an overall consensus; the very tension between the political patriotism of attachment to any particular Arab country *(wattaniyah)* and the overall attachment to a general Arab nationalism *(qawmiyah)* is too strong to overlook, hence the mostly tentative nature of the various attempts for political unification in the Arab world.

The inadequacy of the social vision, however, is much more pronounced. The Syrian Socialist Ba'ath Party is surely one of the most interesting radical political movements in the Arab world. In its two founders it had a unique combination of the political astuteness of Akhram Hourani and the acute analysis of one of the most sensitive Arab modern thinkers, Michel Aflaq (again, significantly enough, a Christian). But even Aflaq's writings are rather short on questions of social structure: the point is that the Party's rule in Syria has done very little to change the basic traditionalism and quietism of Syrian society.

From archives captured by the Israelis on the Golan Heights during the Six Days War we have now a picture of the social structure of the Ba'ath Party in two districts, Kuneitra and Fiq. The number of members in a district of about 100,000 inhabitants was about 300, surely not a mass mobilisation party. Moreover, the social composition of the membership is heavily weighted in the direction of the traditional elites. For a party that calls itself socialist, it is quite amazing to find that 77 per cent of the members were civil servants, teachers and students, 5 per cent employers, landowners and shopowners, and only 13 per cent are classed as workers and peasants.[27] The implications speak for themselves. Similarly, when the Rector of Al-Azhar University proclaims that 'the most perfect, complete, useful and profound socialism is that prescribed by Islam' (22 December 1961), one sees how deep the social conservatism involved is.

There are numerous levels on which Arab and Jewish nationalism can be compared with each other: both are quite problematical movements, with a history in each case quite different from that, not only of traditional European nationalisms, but also, to a degree, of the new nationalisms of the Third World. Among the burdens they have in common are heritages of distorted social structures; that

[27] A. Ben-Zur, 'The Social Composition of Ba'ath Party Membership in the Kuneitra District', in Zeev Goldberg, ed., *Arab Socialism*, Beit Berl, 1970, pp. 235-43 (in Hebrew).

Zionism was able to combine nationalist goals with a vision of social reconstruction and implement it, gave Israeli society, with all its yet unsolved other problems, the cohesion and integration it possesses. One may hope that Arab nationalism will be similarly successful in achieving a comparable amalgam, but this is still hidden in the mists of future development. A student of comparative nationalism would not be able to overlook the fact that the differences between the two movements have to be attributed to the different ways in which problems of social structure have been approached in both societies. Where a vision and praxis of social transformation is lacking, the question raised by nationalism itself remains unsolved.

# Suggested reading

ALMOND, Gabriel and VERBA, Sidney, *The Civic Culture*. Princeton, Princeton U. Press, 1963.

BENDIX, Reinhard, *Nation-Building and Citizenship: Studies of Our Changing Social Order*. New York, Wiley, 1964.

DEUTSCH, Karl, *Nationalism and Social Communication: An Inquiry into the Foundations of Nationality*. 2nd edn, Cambridge, Mass., MIT Press, 1966.

DEUTSCH, Karl W. and FOLTZ, William J. (eds), *Nation-Building*. New York, Atherton, 1963.

HAY, Denys, *Europe: the Emergence of an Idea*. Edinburgh, Edinburgh U. Press, 1957; New York, Harper & Row, 1966.

HAYES, Carlton J.H., *Essays on Nationalism*. New York, Macmillan, 1926.

HAYES, Carlton J.H. *The Historical Evolution of Modern Nationalism*. New York, Richard Smith, 1931.

HAYES, Carlton J.H. *Nationalism: A Religion*. New York, Macmillan, 1960.

HERTZ, Friedrich O., *Nationality in History and Politics: A Study of the Psychology and Sociology of National Sentiment and Character*. London, Kegan Paul, Trench Trubner, 1944.

KEDOURIE, Elie, *Nationalism*. London, Hutchinson, 1960.

KEDOURIE, Elie (ed.), *Nationalism in Asia and Africa*. London, Weidenfeld & Nicolson, 1971.

KOHN, Hans, *The Idea of Nationalism*. New York, Macmillan, 1945.

MINOGUE, K.R., *Nationalism*. London, Batsford, 1967.

ROYAL INSTITUTE OF INTERNATIONAL AFFAIRS, *Nationalism: A Report by a Study Group of Members of the Institute*. London, Oxford U. Press, 1939.

SHAFER, Boyd C., *Faces of Nationalism: New Realities and Old Myths*. New York, Harcourt Brace Jovanovich, 1972. Contains a useful annotated bibliography.

SMITH, Anthony D., *Theories of Nationalism*. London, Duckworth 1971.

SNYDER, Louis (ed.), *The Dynamics of Nationalism: Readings in Its Meaning and Development*. Princeton, Van Nostrand, 1964.

ZNANIECKI, Florian, *Modern Nationalities: A Sociological Study*. Urbana, U. of Illinois Press, 1952.

# Notes on the contributors

Shlomo Avineri, Professor of Political Theory in the Hebrew University of Jerusalem and Director of that University's Levi Eshkol Institute for Economic Social and Political Research, was Visiting Fellow in the History of Ideas Unit in the Australian National University from July to October 1972. Professor Avineri was born in Silesia in 1933 and educated in Israel, taking his doctorate in the Hebrew University in 1964. He has published numerous articles on Marx, on Hegel and on social and political developments in Israel; his books include *The Social and Political Thought of Karl Marx* (1968), *Hegel's Theory of the Modern State* (1972), the selection *Karl Marx on Colonialism and Modernization* (1968) and a Hebrew translation of Karl Marx's early writings. He has also edited and contributed to *Israel and the Palestinians: Reflections on the Clash of Two National Movements* (1971).

Eugene Kamenka is Foundation Professor in the History of Ideas in the Australian National University. Born in Cologne, Germany, in 1928, he was educated in Australia, at the Sydney Technical High School, Sydney University and the Australian National University. He has lived in Israel, England and Singapore and has spent a year as a visiting research worker in the Faculty of Philosophy in Moscow State University. His books include *The Ethical Foundations of Marxism* (1962, 1972), *Marxism and Ethics* (1969) and *The Philosophy of Ludwig Feuerbach* (1970); he has edited *A World in Revolution?* (1970), *Paradigm for Revolution? – The Paris Commune 1871-1971* (1972), *Feudalism, Capitalism and Beyond* (1975) and *The Portable Karl Marx* (forthcoming).

Francis Xavier Martin, Professor of Medieval History in University College, Dublin and a member of the Royal Irish Academy, was born in County Kerry in 1922 and educated at University College, Dublin, the Gregorian University, Rome, and Peterhouse, Cambridge. He joined the Augustinian order in 1941. Professor Martin has written extensively on medieval, Renaissance and Counter-Reformation subjects and on modern Irish history; he is editor of the medieval series of the Dublin Historical Association booklets and one of the three editors of the projected nine-volume history of Ireland sponsored by the Irish government. His books include *Giles of Viterbo 1469-1532: A Renaissance Problem* (1960), *Friar Nugent, Agent of the Counter-Reformation 1569-1635* (1962) and

(with T.W. Moody) *The Course of Irish History* (1967); he has edited
*The Irish Volunteers 1913-1915* (1963), *The Howth Gun-Running 1914*
(1964), *1916 and University College* (1966) and *Leaders and Men of the
Easter Rising: Dublin 1916* (1967). He was Visiting Fellow at La Trobe
University from March to July 1972.

George L. Mosse, Professor of History in the University of Wisconsin
and co-editor of *The Journal of Contemporary History*, was Visiting
Fellow in the History of Ideas Unit in the Australian National University
from June to August 1972. He was born in Berlin in 1918, educated in
Germany, England and the United States and took his Ph.D. at Harvard.
His books include *The Holy Pretence, The Culture of Western Europe,
Nazi Culture, The Reformation, The Crisis of German Ideology, Germans
and Jews* and *The Nationalization of the Masses*. He has been Visiting
Professor at Stanford University and is a permanent Visiting Professor
at the Hebrew University of Jerusalem; he is currently completing a
book on the history of racism in Europe.

John Plamenatz, Chichele Professor of Social and Political Theory in the
University of Oxford and Fellow of All Souls College, was Visiting Fellow in the History of Ideas Unit, Australian National University from
July to September 1972. Professor Plamenatz, born in Montenegro in
1912, came to England in 1919 and was educated at Oriel College,
Oxford. His publications include *Consent, Freedom and Political Obli-
gation* (1938), *English Utilitarians* (1950), *The Revolutionary Movement
in France 1815-71* (1952), *From Marx to Stalin* (1953), *German Marxism
and Russian Communism* (1954), *On Alien Rule and Self-Government*
(1960), *Man and Society*, Vols. I and II (1963) and *Ideology* (1970).
Professor Plamenatz died in 1975.

Wang Gungwu, Professor of Far Eastern History in the Australian
National University, was born in Surabaya in 1930 and educated in
Malaya, the National Central University in Nanking, China, the University
of Malaya in Singapore and the School of Oriental and African Studies
in London, where he took his doctorate with a thesis in Chinese history.
He has taught in Singapore and been Professor of History in the Univer-
sity of Malaya (Kuala Lumpur). Professor Wang has published numerous
articles on Chinese and South-East Asian history; his books include *A
Short History of the Nanyang Chinese* (1959), *The Nanhai Trade: A
History of Early Chinese Trade in the South China Sea* (1961) and *The
Structure of Power in North China during the Five Dynasties* (1963).

# Index